WHAT YOUR COLLEAGUES ARE SAYING . . .

We are in a place in history where we desperately need answers to questions that will determine the future of our nation's most precious possession—our children. *The Distance Learning Playbook* is an incredible resource with a wealth of practical support for teachers and administrators, and it will fill a huge information gap that many schools are experiencing in educating students from a distance. With very practical, easy-to-use examples of how to start and end a class, provide the social-emotional support needed, and set up norms to develop a safe culture for students to learn at high levels, this is a must-have for educators at all levels— district leaders, principals, coaches, and teachers. This resource is ideal for schools that are looking for answers in the quest to create a whole-child approach to virtual education.

—**Dr. Charles Newman,** Assistant Superintendent
of Educational Services, Perris Union High School District, CA

Never has there been another time in history where the majority of educators around the world jumped into action to reinvent how schools and classrooms function. Using current research of what constitutes best practice, *The Distance Learning Playbook* helps guide us all through "pandemic teaching." This book is filled with ideas and insight from real educators as they reflect on what they themselves need and what students will need to learn within a new teaching and learning environment. Douglas Fisher, Nancy Frey, and John Hattie continue to develop relational pedagogies that support cultural responsiveness and social emotional development in order to have a positive effect on student achievement, but this time, in a new setting. They help us understand research-based approaches to engage every student, and in doing so, help us select the appropriate digital tools. I can't wait to use this book in our professional learning.

—**Lisa Riggs,** Assistant Superintendent of Curriculum,
Instruction and Assessment, Gresham-Barlow School District, OR

I love this book! It provides practical information to support *all* our teachers as they shift all or some of their instruction to distance learning. It is the best of what Douglas Fisher, Nancy Frey, and John Hattie have to teach us about great instruction, all in a hands-on tool to guide teachers as they plan for the upcoming year. From teacher self-care to feedback, assessment, and grading, it's all addressed here. This resource is right on time and will be a foundational tool to help shape the instructional focus at my school this year.

—**Jennifer Carr,** Principal, Ahwahnee Middle School, Fresno, CA

As we charter the unfamiliar territory of a blended learning platform, we turn to the experts who have gone before us. Douglas Fisher, Nancy Frey, and John Hattie remind us that the focus is not technology, learning management systems, or devices, but that the focus remains student learning. This book serves as a safe haven, as it reminds us what effective teaching and learning entail, and then wraps it around a digital learning framework. Whether districts are familiar with distance learning or starting from ground zero, *The Distance Learning Playbook* is the place to start.

—**Melanie Spence,** K–12 Curriculum Coordinator/Assistant Principal
and Education Consultant, Sloan-Hendrix School District, Imboden, AR

Echoing through the pages of this timely book is this message: *effective teaching is effective teaching, no matter where it occurs.* Teacher voices and classroom examples animate core principles of research-based teaching and learning, enabling the reader to visualize practices in both face-to-face and online learning environments. Multiple self-assessments and templates for reflection support reader interaction with the content. The authors connect Visible Learning and informed teacher decision-making to all facets of effective lesson design and delivery and address the important issues of equity and inclusiveness, learner self-regulation, and the use of formative evaluation and feedback to move learning forward. A must-read book!

—**Jackie Acree Walsh,** Author of *Quality Questioning, Second Edition* and Consultant, Montgomery, AL

The year 2020 will be forever etched in our minds as the Era of Distance Learning. The COVID-19 pandemic has caused cascading changes that have shifted our educational institutions. This concerted seismic move has elevated the need for robust internet connections and meaningful virtual interactions. *The Distance Learning Playbook* is an invaluable resource designed to prepare our teachers to provide a powerful learning environment through technology, while promoting the most powerful tool available to educators—a caring relationship with students.

—**Dr. Francisco Escobedo,** Superintendent of Chula Vista Elementary School District, CA

THE
DISTANCE
LEARNING
PLAYBOOK GRADES K-12

TEACHING FOR **ENGAGEMENT** & **IMPACT** IN ANY SETTING

THE DISTANCE LEARNING PLAYBOOK GRADES K–12

DOUGLAS FISHER · NANCY FREY · JOHN HATTIE

CORWIN

FOR INFORMATION:

Corwin

A SAGE Company

2455 Teller Road

Thousand Oaks, California 91320

(800) 233-9936

www.corwin.com

SAGE Publications Ltd.

1 Oliver's Yard

55 City Road

London EC1Y 1SP

United Kingdom

SAGE Publications India Pvt. Ltd.

B 1/I 1 Mohan Cooperative Industrial Area

Mathura Road, New Delhi 110 044

India

SAGE Publications Asia-Pacific Pte. Ltd.

18 Cross Street #10-10/11/12

China Square Central

Singapore 048423

Director and Publisher, Corwin Classroom: Lisa Luedeke

Editorial Development Manager: Julie Nemer

Associate Content Development Editor: Sharon Wu

Production Editor: Melanie Birdsall

Copy Editor: Diane DiMura

Typesetter: C&M Digitals (P) Ltd.

Proofreader: Sally Jaskold

Indexer: Molly Hall

Cover Designer: Gail Buschman

Interior Designer: Rose Storey

Marketing Manager: Deena Meyer

Module-opening images courtesy of iStock.com/Eoneren

Printed in the United States of America

ISBN 978-1-0718-2892-2

Library of Congress Control Number: 2020910532

This book is printed on acid-free paper.

20 21 22 23 24 10 9 8 7 6 5 4

CONTENTS

Visit the companion website at
resources.corwin.com/distancelearningplaybook
for downloadable resources and videos.

LIST OF VIDEOS

Note From the Publisher: The authors have provided video and web content throughout the book that is available to you through QR (quick response) codes. To read a QR code, you must have a smartphone or tablet with a camera. We recommend that you download a QR code reader app that is made specifically for your phone or tablet brand.

Videos may also be accessed at **resources.corwin.com/distancelearningplaybook**

ACKNOWLEDGMENTS

This playbook was the brainchild of Elena Nikitina at Corwin, who proposed the original idea that energized us all. This book would not exist without the tireless efforts of our amazing editor, Lisa Luedeke, who mobilized the collective effort needed to bring it to life. We are grateful to both of you for your vision and can-do attitude.

INTRODUCTION

The grammar of schooling has changed. And it changed quickly. There is an expectation that students will learn from a distance. That learning may be fully at a distance or a blend of online and brick-and-mortar schools. Who knows what school will be like in the short term? And we hope that we return better than before, taking ideas that we implemented during pandemic teaching and applying them in new situations. The constant, however, remains the same: to ensure that students are learning. We suspect that the future will include increased amounts of distance learning. Teachers have embraced their responsibility to impact learning, irrespective of the format of school. Let's seize on what we have learned to improve schooling in any format, whether face-to-face or from a distance.

Teachers are amazing and the public is realizing this in substantial ways. Unlike parents with a couple of kids in their homes, teachers have twenty to forty students at once. These educators can motivate students (mostly) to engage in activities that make the struggle of learning joyful. Teachers provide feedback at the right time and in the right way to each student and teachers do not "do" the work for the students. Teachers know where to go next and how to balance the breadth and depth of the ever-varied school curriculum. They utilize their know-how to invest in the after schoolwork of grading, preparing lessons, developing resources, and going to professional learning and meetings. We lost count of the number of parents who posted on social media that they had no idea how their child's teacher was able to accomplish all that they did. As one parent said, "I had a hard time motivating and supervising my own child. His teacher makes it look so easy, and she has twenty-five others in the class at the same time."

But the world changed in early 2020. And we'd like to take a moment to acknowledge the heroic efforts of educators worldwide who, during a pandemic, used what they knew to create meaningful learning opportunities for students. They didn't miss a beat. Like the health-care workers who rose to the challenge, teachers stepped up and made sure that students continued to learn. We didn't say that it was easy. And we didn't say that we wanted to learn this way. But learn we did. And now that we did learn, it's time to plan for distance learning using what we know now.

To be clear, the pandemic teaching of 2020 was really not distance learning. It was also not homeschooling, which is a choice parents make for very specific reasons (e.g., religious, safety, not happy with their public school). It was crisis teaching. Now, we have time to be more purposeful and intentional with distance

Doug Fisher introduces the goals of this book.

To read a QR code, you must have a smartphone or tablet with a camera. We recommend that you download a QR code reader app that is made specifically for your phone or tablet brand.

learning. What should not be lost is that as a field we learned more about what works by at times experiencing what didn't work in a virtual setting. It heightened our sense of what we already knew in face-to-face classrooms (Hattie, 2018):

- Fostering student self-regulation is crucial for moving learning to deep and transfer levels.

- Learning accelerates when the student, not the teacher, is taught to be in control of learning.

- There needs to be a diversity of instructional approaches (not just some direct instruction and then some off-line independent work).

- Well-designed peer learning impacts understanding.

- Feedback in a high-trust environment must be integrated into the learning cycle.

Let's use what we have learned and are continuing to learn whether in a face-to-face or distance learning environment. As a part of face-to-face teaching, let's build our students' capacity (and our own) for distance learning. Now we have time to use evidence about what works best to impact students. And that's the purpose of this book—to apply the wisdom of Visible Learning® research to distance learning. But before we do so, we need to acknowledge the potential differential impact of distance learning on students.

TO BE CLEAR, THE PANDEMIC TEACHING OF 2020 WAS REALLY NOT DISTANCE LEARNING. IT WAS CRISIS TEACHING.

A VISIBLE LEARNING® PRIMER

There exists a significant amount of published research about education, and more studies are produced each year. Who doesn't want to make research- or evidence-based decisions about teaching and learning? It's hard to sift through to figure out what to do. It seems that everything "works" so any choice we make seems reasonable. But the fact of the matter is that some things work best. Thus, it's useful to know what works best to accelerate students' learning.

Enter the Visible Learning database. It's easily accessible at www.visiblelearningmetax.com. This database focuses on meta-analyses, or aggregations of studies, to determine the impact that specific actions or influences have on students' learning. These meta-analyses use an effect size, which is a statistical tool to scale the impact. To date, the database includes over 1,800 meta-analyses with over 300 million students. The average impact on students' learning from all the things we do is 0.40 (effect size). Thus, influences over 0.40 are above average and should accelerate students' learning. Those below are less likely to ensure that students learn a full year of stuff for a year of school. That does not mean we ignore those influences below

0.40, but rather we are cautious and we think about ways that we implement those practices.

Let's consider a few examples. Are you surprised that a students' prior achievement is related to their future achievement? The effect size is 0.59. Yes, students who have achieved in the past are likely to achieve in the future. The database confirms what we expect. Are you surprised that boredom has a negative effect on learning? The effect size is -0.47. Learning opportunities are lost when students are bored. There is a logic to the evidence summarized in the Visible Learning database, right?

As another example, the instructional strategy jigsaw has an effect size of 1.20. Powerful! It should work to accelerate student learning. Our personal experiences with this approach, when implemented correctly, confirm it. But, since we are talking about distance learning, it's important to note that none of the jigsaw studies collected for any of the meta-analyses were done from afar. In this case, we'll have to take a leap of faith and identify the essential components of a jigsaw and determine how it can be used online.

Several themes are at the heart of Visible Learning.

1. **The first is that investment in learning means that there is a drive to foster each student's increasing ability to recognize when they are learning, when they are not, and how to go about fixing it.** That means that teacher clarity and feedback are crucial. You will find separate modules devoted to these two things elsewhere in this book.

2. **The second theme is that teachers know the impact of their instruction in terms of progress and achievement and take steps to refine their approaches.** That means that we have methods for discovering what students already know in order to minimize wasted instructional time such that we can focus on needed learning experiences. Further, the individual student is the unit of analysis—we know what works, what works when, and what works for whom.

3. **The third theme is that the mindframes of teachers, which is to say dispositions and beliefs, are in the driver's seat.** That means that we collaborate with one another, talk about learning more than teaching, and invest in relationships with children and adults in order to be an agent of change.

These themes transcend the delivery method. Whether face-to-face with students or in virtual or distance environments, these themes endure. Take a few minutes to reflect on these themes and note how you accomplish these in face-to-face environments. Then consider what these might look like in virtual spaces.

Vince Bustamante talks about the Visible Learning database.

DISTANCE LEARNING IS NOT AN ACCELERATOR. IT'S ALSO NOT NEGATIVE. THAT MEANS THAT THE SETTING ISN'T THE DECIDING FACTOR.

NOTE TO SELF

How do you enact these themes in face-to-face classrooms? How can they occur in virtual classrooms?

THEME	FACE-TO-FACE SETTINGS	VIRTUAL/DISTANCE SETTINGS
Teacher clarity and feedback is used to fuel students' ability to become their own teachers (they are assessment-capable learners).		
Methods for measuring the impact of teaching are used to understand each student's progress *and* achievement, with adjustments to teaching made accordingly.		
Investment in collaboration with adults and relationships with students is continuous.		

 Available for download at **resources.corwin.com/distancelearningplaybook**

VISIBLE LEARNING AND DISTANCE LEARNING

This brings us to the effect size of distance learning itself. We know the effect size of technology remains low and has been so for the last fifty years. As Dylan Wiliam has often said, technology is the revolution that is still coming! The effect of distance learning is small (0.14) but that does not mean it is NOT effective—it means it does not matter whether teachers undertake teaching in situ or from a distance over the internet (or, like when John started in his first university, via the post office). What we *do* matters, not the medium of doing it.

There are some technology elements that are worth attending to. The highest effects of digital technology are interactive videos (0.54), intelligent tutoring systems (0.51), in writing (0.42), and in mathematics (0.35). The lowest effects are the presence of mobile phones (at −0.34, please turn them off), and the presence of one-on-one laptops (0.16). Of course, the studies that were used to calculate the effect sizes involved purposeful and planned learning in virtual or distance environments and in face-to-face classrooms, not crisis pandemic teaching.

When people see that there is an effect size of 0.14, they incorrectly assume that distance learning is not effective. But let's take a closer look. In comparison with traditional building-based learning, distance learning is not an accelerator. It's also not negative. That means that the setting isn't the deciding factor. Nor should it be interpreted that "distance is disastrous." What is far more important are the methods of teaching that spark learning, not the medium. Consider what some of those technologies with higher effect sizes have to offer. Interactive videos require students to engage in active learning, not just passive viewing (something students do in classrooms, too). Intelligent tutoring systems provide rapid feedback and customized instruction based on what the learner knows and doesn't know. Similarly, high-performing classroom teachers use responsive feedback and instruction that reduces teaching what is already known in favor of what needs to be known next.

The choice of task matters critically. It is the choice of tasks relative to where students are now and where they need to go next that advances their learning.

- Use technology for great diagnosis of what students need to learn.

- Share scoring rubrics and success criteria up front with students before they get too involved in the task.

- Be clear. Teacher clarity matters more when students are not in front of you to correct, cajole, and to give instant feedback. You cannot immediately evaluate progress as you do the physical classroom.

- Build formative evaluation opportunities into the tasks.

John Hattie talks about distance learning.

IT IS THE CHOICE OF TASKS RELATIVE TO WHERE STUDENTS ARE NOW AND WHERE THEY NEED TO GO NEXT THAT ADVANCES THEIR LEARNING.

TECHNOLOGY
USE IS THE
MEANS AND
STARTING POINT,
NOT THE CORE,
OF TEACHING.

We need to view technology use like planning lessons and creating resources: It is the means and starting point, not the core, of teaching. It is the decisions we make as students are learning, as we listen to them think aloud, as we give them alternate strategies and help them work with others to jointly advance learning, as we formatively evaluate our impact, that are important.

- Optimize the social interaction aspects (we do not want to be talked at, but learn with).
- Check for understanding (listen to the feedback from the students about their learning even more when you do not have the usual cues of the classrooms).
- Make sure there is a balance between the precious knowledge and the deep thinking (too often online favors the former over the latter).

Bottom line: Understand what it means to be a learner online. When the usual peer interactions are often not as present, the teacher's observational skills are different, and there is too often an overemphasis on content and repetition.

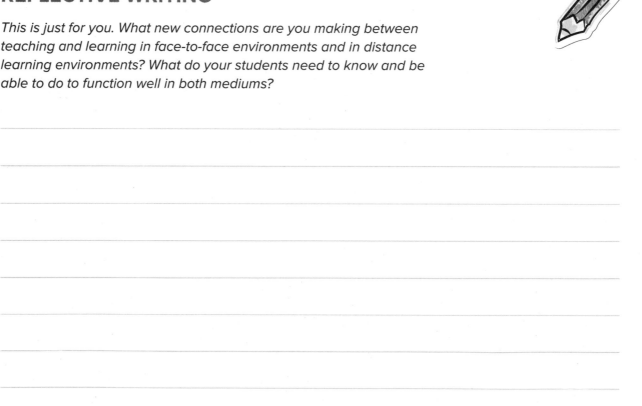

REFLECTIVE WRITING

This is just for you. What new connections are you making between teaching and learning in face-to-face environments and in distance learning environments? What do your students need to know and be able to do to function well in both mediums?

A QUESTION OF EQUITY

Students whose learning has been traditionally compromised in schools remain at risk in distance learning. This includes English learners; students with disabilities; students who live in poverty; those from traditionally underrepresented ethnic and racial groups; students who identify as gay, lesbian, bisexual, or transgender; and those who have experienced significant trauma. Teachers and school systems should redouble their efforts to ensure that the needs of these students are met. The San Diego County Office of Education identified three distance learning equity needs:

Nicole Law talks about the equity challenges associated with distance learning.

- Meet students' basic needs.

- Ensure equitable access to learning resources.

- Proactively design responsive, restorative structures.

They have developed a list of actions for each of these needs, and the list of resources for each action, which is regularly updated, can be found here: https://bit.ly/2A55c1j

But there are students who may not have been considered in the past who are also at risk when it comes to distance learning, including students

- Who struggle with low self-regulation and are highly dependent on the teacher

- Who return with high levels of stress and social and emotional concerns and possible resulting behavioral issues

- With limited proficiency in using quality learning strategies and guidance necessary to promote development

- Who already had a lack of progress in school for whatever reason

- Who have low concepts of themselves as learners

- Who lack proficiency in the critical reading and numeracy skills needed to move to the next level—particularly in the primary grades, and are thus more likely to become part of the "Matthew effect" in which the rich get richer while the poor get poorer (Stanovich, 1986)

- Living in homes that are not safe (for many of these students, school is the safe haven); there will be an exacerbation of physical and emotional health issues

- With parents who have limited capacity or desire to engage them in the schoolwork at home and who ignore or permit no engagement with schoolwork

All students, and especially those who are at greater risk of not making expected progress, must be targeted for proactive supports that address their equity needs and build their capacity to learn at a distance. Throughout this book, we

Nancy Frey delivers a message to educators.

include examples of ways that teachers can address the needs of these students and work to ensure that the equity gains that have been realized are not lost. In addition, we see distance learning as an opportunity to engage students in different ways and potentially address some of the needs that they have that could not have been met in traditional classes. We want to promote the notion that what we have learned through the research evidence of distance learning (not just our recent emergency efforts) should be leveraged to improve teaching in virtual environments. We also want to advocate that what we have learned through the research evidence on learning in any environment should inform our future efforts and improve our readiness, as well as our students' capacity, to continue their education regardless of the setting.

You are still an educator. You didn't forget how to teach. You can still impact the lives of your students and know that you made a difference. We hope that this playbook provides you with examples of familiar tasks and ideas that you can mobilize at a distance to ensure students learn.

MODULE 1

TAKE CARE
OF YOURSELF

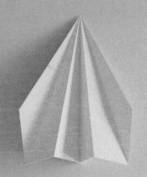

LEARNING INTENTIONS

- I am learning to take care of myself as I engage with my students.

- I am learning about the impact of trauma on educators.

Perhaps you're surprised that we start a book about distance learning with the recommendation that you need to take care of yourself. But hear us out. If you burn out, if you become exhausted and overwhelmed, you're no good to your students (much less your family, friends, let alone yourself). The vast majority of us did not sign up for this type of teaching. We had images of ourselves arriving at a school building to be greeted by the faces of eager learners who could not wait to see us. There would be start times, breaks (called passing periods and recess), lunches, conversations with colleagues, and a signal that the workday was finished. Of course, we might choose to take some work home with us, perhaps to plan or grade, but there was a separation between work and home. Distance learning can interrupt all of those routines. So, before we engage in distance learning, we need to take care of ourselves. As our friend and colleague Ricky Robertson reminds us, follow the instructions of the flight attendant and put your oxygen mask on first before helping others.

You'll find that in each module in this playbook, we invite you first to draw on your own expertise. Although you may be new to distance learning, you aren't new to education. You have been a student and now you are a teacher, instructional coach, or school leader. And prior knowledge, which is an aspect of prior achievement, has a strong influence on new learning if it is properly leveraged. In fact, learning strategies that integrate prior knowledge with new learning have a strong influence, with an effect size of 0.93 (Hattie, 2018). Consider this an invitation to activate your prior knowledge to develop new ideas.

DRAWING ON MY EXPERTISE

How do you maintain a work-life balance? How can you do so when working from home? How do you do so when working at school?

For the vast majority of us, our first experience at distance learning started as a result of the global pandemic COVID-19. This book is not just about that. It's about developing and delivering quality distance learning experiences for students—anywhere, anytime. But we would be remiss if we did not acknowledge the initiation of this type of teaching. Who could have imagined that we would be sheltering in place, anxious about a monster that could harm us or our loved ones? But the current crisis is just the most recent, albeit major, trauma we have experienced. Unlike other traumatic experiences, this one is global and has touched every member of the human race. There is some comfort in that but it's still difficult and surreal. It also makes us stop to think about the other traumas we have experienced. You see, trauma is not just something that happens to "them"—our students or other people. It's hard to imagine a person who has reached the age of 25 who hasn't experienced at least one adverse childhood event:

- Divorce

- Death of a loved one

- A loved one incarcerated

- Community violence

- Poverty

- Exposure to domestic violence

- Living with someone who has mental illness or who is suicidal

- Alcohol or drug addiction in the home

We carry that trauma with us. As Van der Kolk noted in the title of his 2015 book, "The body keeps the score." By that, he meant that traumatic experiences inevitably leave their traces on our minds, emotions, and even on our physical health. We all have those traces and some of us have yet to address the impact. That's why social and emotional learning needs to continue with adults and does not end upon graduation from high school. And, as we noted earlier, additional traumatic experiences accumulate throughout our lives.

It's important to acknowledge the issue. An ostrich approach is not useful. Instead, schools can engage in social and emotional learning for adults, if for no other reason but the fact that teachers model behaviors that students mimic. When we model healthy, growth-producing relationships, students see how they work. When we model respect, kindness, and a range of emotions, students notice how we regulate and respond. But even more importantly, we believe, is the opportunity to help adults continue their social and emotional learning journey and become happier, healthier members of the community, both at school and in the wider community.

ALTHOUGH YOU MAY BE NEW TO DISTANCE LEARNING, YOU AREN'T NEW TO EDUCATION.

Yes, that got deep, but we want to recognize that trauma is part of our lives and don't want to exacerbate it during distance learning efforts. There are a number of recommendations, based on evidence from other stressful times in the lives of humans as well as long-term "work at home" studies, that we can use to inform, and take care of, ourselves. We will chunk these into some groups and provide you an opportunity to consider your plan. The first is about your workspace at home. The recommendations are to

TRAUMA IS PART OF OUR LIVES, AND WE DON'T WANT TO EXACERBATE IT DURING DISTANCE LEARNING EFFORTS.

- Keep a dedicated workspace

- Set ground rules with the people in your space

The dedicated office space does not have to be a home office. That's not what we mean. But rather, a place where you can easily teach and engage students. Brittini Glass set up a space in her apartment, in the corner of her kitchen.

As she said, "I like the light here and when I'm done working, I can leave the kitchen and go to another area of my apartment away from work." Ms. Glass has all of her supplies in a rolling file cabinet near the small table that she uses to hold her computer. She has a light behind the computer that highlights her face so that students can see her better. Ms. Glass adds, "I also have familiar items from the classroom behind me on a shelf so that it looks a little more like school when we are live."

Mike Perez has set up a place in his unfinished basement. Like Ms. Glass, he has all of his supplies at the ready. He has a standing desk to avoid sitting all day. "When I'm talking with students, I'm used to standing. This just feels more natural to me," he says. "I think I project better when I stand and I'm amazed at how much they watch me. I don't talk the whole time, but when I do, I prefer to stand."

Kameron Warfield talks about her dedicated workspace.

In addition to having a dedicated space in your living environment to teach, it's important to set the ground rules with the others who live in the home. Of course, we all understand the child who needs something and interrupts a live class meeting or the pet that jumps up on the table and walks in front of the computer. It's just that your stress level can be reduced when you have clear guidelines for people. Ms. Glass asks that people in her home text her to let her know that they're coming into the kitchen so she is not surprised. Mr. Perez asks his family not to play around his workspace so that things are not moved. He also asks that they wash clothes on the weekend or in the evening so that the machines are not running while he is working.

NOTE TO SELF

My dedicated workspace is

I need to have the following items near me:

My virtual background is a blank wall, a picture of my regular class, something not too distracting for my students.

Guidelines that I need to share with others when working from home include

-
-
-
-
-
-
-

The second group of recommendations focuses on routines and includes that you

- Create a morning routine
- Maintain regular hours
- Schedule breaks
- End your day with a routine

Routines are useful for us as they help us organize, plan, and predict. One of the risks with distance learning is that our routines are disrupted, and we are not sure how to re-establish them. In future modules, we'll focus on routines for students. For now, we need to focus on the routines for us, the educators.

As an example of establishing routines, Stephany Cardenas walks early each morning and then has breakfast with her family. She has scheduled breaks in her day that mirror the schedule she had previously. She takes twenty minutes mid-morning for recess, forty-five minutes for lunch, and then a short stretch break in the afternoon. She ends her workday by sending a summary email to her students, thanking them for their work for the day and reminding them about the learning for the next day. Ms. Cardenas also has a routine for the end of her day, which is to either read or meditate. As she says, "I take about 20 minutes each night for some alone time. I'm an avid reader, so that's calming for me. But a few days per week, I like to mediate and just sit quietly and let my mind go. Then I'm ready to sleep and am eager for the next day."

Claudia Readwright is an instructional coach in the Fresno Unified School District in California, specializing in primary education.

Brian Kennedy shares his morning routines and his schedule.

By Claudia Readwright

A VIEW FROM THE EARLY YEARS

We have been invited to activate our prior knowledge in order to develop new ideas. I thought it prudent to take a lesson from the Mister Roger's playbook. If we employ a visual cue that signals the beginning and ending of our workday, it can serve as a reminder to our children and ourselves. Mister Rogers enters his "television house," removes and hangs up his jacket, then changes out of his street shoes into his sneakers. Our own routines should similarly aid us in bracketing our workdays. Apply your early learning lens to yourself, as you know how important it is to continue our own social and emotional learning journey.

Routines make children feel welcome and included, and the same applies to us as adults. Striking yoga poses or other gentle movement activities, accompanied by peaceful music, is a way to engage with yourself first thing in the morning. Other early morning routines might include a short walk, a few quiet minutes outside on your porch or balcony, or listening to a favorite podcast while you get ready.

Some of the "Work at Home" recommendations are easy enough to implement and echo what we teach our own students. How might you set up a dedicated workspace? Maybe that could include a trifold science board created to look like the mini focus board you have in your physical classroom. It could include an emotions poster, a number line, 5 and 10 frames, an alphabet frieze, and the current art print for discussion. It is a manageable size, portable, and can be folded flat if needed. Having your daily teaching items easily available to you can lower your stress level when teaching online.

How might we establish ground rules in our shared space? Your family and your pets are an important part of your life, just as they are for the children we teach. Set up a signal with your family that shows when you'll be teaching in a live session—perhaps a kind note on the door. A hat or crown reminds others this is a time for no interruptions (barring emergencies, of course). And if a family member or pet wanders into the camera frame, anyway, introduce them. You're modeling for your own students how we handle unexpected interruptions in ways that are graceful and kind.

Four focus areas have given our early learning team time to reflect and steer our self-care efforts in a positive direction. For a Health benefit, try including at least forty minutes of daily exercise, three days a week. In the Love category, include doing something just for you. By stepping out of your comfort zone, and trying something new, you can gain a sense of Competence. If we focus on demonstrating our thankfulness, we may notice our Gratitude quotient grows. In addition, weekly check-ins with colleagues are often productive in sharing common challenges and generating new ideas.

Close your workday with an emotional check-in. Celebrate what you have accomplished and set a small goal for tomorrow. Remember that making each day special for children starts with you being you. Then hang up your cardigan for the day and know that you've done well.

NOTE TO SELF

MY MORNING ROUTINE OPTIONS	WHEN I WILL TAKE BREAKS	MY END-OF-DAY ROUTINE OPTIONS

Now, highlight one morning routine option and one end-of-day routine and try them for two weeks. If it's not helping you, change it up and try something else. But for the sake of your family, your students, and your well-being, find some routines that work and use them regularly.

The third group of recommendations focuses on socialization opportunities. We are professionals, and professionals socialize with other professionals. There are a number of options for doing this, including online and off-line activities. When we are teaching at a distance, we need to remember that we need to socialize with people outside of our homes and keep actively engaged in our friend networks. We thrive on both personal and professional connections and we should not forget this necessity as we teach from a distance. Thus, you should consider opportunities to

- Socialize with colleagues
- Have a connected and meaningful conversation each day with someone outside of your home

Chrissy Thompson committed to attend one online professional learning event per month so that she could stay connected with others in her profession. As she said, "I want to feel part of something larger. It started with an online book club. I wasn't sure that I would like it, but the conversation with people all over the world, especially in the breakout rooms, was amazing and energizing for me. So, I do something online with the profession each month. I get so many great ideas and I just really like the interactions I get to have with other educators. At my school, we have weekly team meetings, which are also great. But these wider opportunities make me feel connected."

Armando Hueso made a commitment to have at least one conversation per day with someone outside of his family. As he says, "I take a coffee break every day and talk with someone. Sometimes it's people from my school but sometimes it's others. I schedule it so that we're both free. I like video calls, but some people prefer voice only calls. These conversations are important for me and they keep me grounded. I see friends and such but because I'm not at a school building, I miss the connections with my colleagues. These coffee breaks meet that need for me."

Your turn. Take a look at the prompt on the next page—how will you socialize with colleagues and ensure that you have one meaningful, connected conversation each day with someone outside of your home?

In addition to the three groups of personal support discussed above, it's important for people to take care of themselves physically. Without sounding too touchy-feely or reinforcing stereotypes about Southern California or Australia (where we live), managing our stress, eating healthily, and exercising regularly are important to our well-being. For example, Sharla Green says, "I was feeling a little stressed when I started distance learning. No, actually, a lot stressed. My friend recommended an app for me, but I didn't try it. My stress kept increasing and another person asked why I bit her head off, so I decided I needed to do something. I use an app called Pacifica but there are lots of them out there. I'm better for it and my students have even noticed that I'm calmer in class."

NOTE TO SELF

My social connection plan includes

Your turn. What can you do to support your well-being?

NOTE TO SELF

My plan for stress management:

_____

_____

_____

_____

My plan for healthy eating:

_____

_____

_____

_____

_____

My plan for getting regular sleep:

_____

_____

_____

_____

My exercise plan:

_____

_____

_____

_____

_____

 Available for download at **resources.corwin.com/distancelearningplaybook**

See, it wasn't that hard. But we know that developing a wellness plan is only part of it. Having a commitment partner increases the likelihood that you will actually implement your plans. Angelica Chavez was very honest about this. As she said, she had a lot of plans in her mind and sometimes they were even written out. But they were rarely implemented. When she learned about the value of commitment partners, she contacted another teacher on her grade level and asked if they could check in with each other each week. "I knew that I would have to answer to Pam," Ms. Chavez said, "so I would really do it. But it turns out, I really like what I decided to do and was super happy to talk with her and share my success. I don't know what I was waiting for all of those years. If I had only known."

It's your turn. Who could serve as your commitment partner and what would you ask of that person?

Kristen Speck talks about her stress management techniques.

My commitment partner is	
I need the following from this person:	
We will check in	☐ Daily
	☐ Two times per week
	☐ Three times per week
	☐ Weekly
	☐ Biweekly

 Available for download at **resources.corwin.com/distancelearningplaybook**

The last area we'd like to focus on, in terms of taking care of yourself, is compassion fatigue. Most of the time, teachers experience compassion satisfaction, which is the pleasure we derive from being able to do our work well (Stamm, 2010). When we feel effective, especially when we see evidence of our students' learning, our compassion satisfaction increases and we enjoy our work.

The other side of this coin is compassion fatigue. Compassion fatigue is a combination of physical, emotional, and spiritual depletion associated with the trauma-related work we do where others are in significant emotional pain or physical distress. It's known as the high cost of caring. As Figley (2002) notes, "Compassion fatigue is a state experienced by those helping people in distress; it is an extreme state of tension and preoccupation with the suffering of those being helped to the degree that it can create a secondary traumatic stress for the helper" (p. 1435). As Elliott, Elliott, and Spears (2018) note,

> Symptoms can develop over a period of years, or after as little as six weeks on the job. Lowered tolerance for frustration, an aversion to working with certain students, and decreased job satisfaction are just a few of the effects that represent a significant risk to job performance as well as to teachers' own personal, emotional, and physical well-being. (p. 29)

The signs of compassion fatigue include

- Isolation

- Emotional outbursts

- Sadness, apathy

- Impulse to rescue anyone in need

- Persistent physical ailments

- Substance abuse

- Hypervigilance or hyperarousal

- Recurring nightmares or flashbacks

- Excessive complaints about colleagues, management, or those being helped

The American Academy of Family Physicians developed a self-assessment tool for health-care workers, which we have adapted for educators (see Figure 1.1). If you have these signs, please seek help. We need you. Your students need you. And compassion fatigue can be overcome.

COMPASSION FATIGUE IS A COMBINATION OF PHYSICAL, EMOTIONAL, AND SPIRITUAL DEPLETION ASSOCIATED WITH THE WORK WE DO WITH OTHERS.

Figure 1.1 Compassion Fatigue Inventory

Personal concerns commonly intrude on my professional role.	Yes	No
My colleagues seem to lack understanding.	Yes	No
I find even small changes enormously draining.	Yes	No
I can't seem to recover quickly after association with trauma.	Yes	No
Association with trauma affects me very deeply.	Yes	No
My students' stress affects me deeply.	Yes	No
I have lost my sense of hopefulness.	Yes	No
I feel vulnerable all the time.	Yes	No
I feel overwhelmed by unfinished personal business.	Yes	No

Source: Used with permission from Overcoming Compassion Fatigue, Apr., 2000, Vol. 7, No. 4, *Family Practice Management.* Copyright © 2000 American Academy of Family Physicians. All rights reserved.

CONCLUSION

We started with a recommendation to take care of yourself. We hope you take this seriously and carefully consider actions you can take. We promise that the rest of the book focuses on teaching and learning in distance learning using the knowledge gained from the Visible Learning database. As a final task for this module, now that you have a sense of what might be involved in taking care of yourself, complete the following self-assessment.

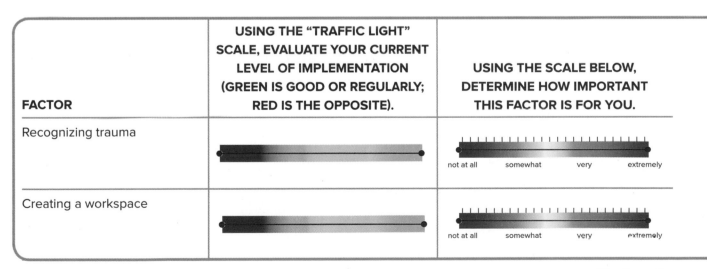

FACTOR	USING THE "TRAFFIC LIGHT" SCALE, EVALUATE YOUR CURRENT LEVEL OF IMPLEMENTATION (GREEN IS GOOD OR REGULARLY; RED IS THE OPPOSITE).	USING THE SCALE BELOW, DETERMINE HOW IMPORTANT THIS FACTOR IS FOR YOU.
Recognizing trauma		not at all somewhat very extremely
Creating a workspace		not at all somewhat very extremely

(Continued)

FACTOR	USING THE "TRAFFIC LIGHT" SCALE, EVALUATE YOUR CURRENT LEVEL OF IMPLEMENTATION (GREEN IS GOOD OR REGULARLY; RED IS THE OPPOSITE).	USING THE SCALE BELOW, DETERMINE HOW IMPORTANT THIS FACTOR IS FOR YOU.
Establishing personal routines		not at all somewhat very extremely
Socializing with others		not at all somewhat very extremely
Managing stress		not at all somewhat very extremely
Eating and sleeping well		not at all somewhat very extremely
Exercising		not at all somewhat very extremely
Finding a commitment partner		not at all somewhat very extremely
Recognizing compassion fatigue		not at all somewhat very extremely

SUCCESS CRITERIA

- I can identify a place to work.

- I can practice my routines and manage my schedule.

- I have at least one connected conversation per day with someone outside of my home.

- I have a plan for my personal well-being.

- I recognize the signs of trauma and compassion fatigue.

MODULE 2

THE FIRST DAYS OF SCHOOL

LEARNING INTENTIONS

- I am learning about classroom norms, routines, and procedures useful in distance learning.

- I am learning about creating virtual and distance learning environments.

The night before the first day of school for students is usually fraught with a mixture of anticipation and anxiety. Who will be in my class? Will my teacher like me? What will I wear? These concerns mirror those of teachers: We look forward to meeting our new students, we want them to like us, and we pick out our new outfit to make a good first impression.

Whether in a distance learning environment or a face-to-face one, starting off the school year on the right foot matters. As Mary Poppins says, "Well begun is half done." Consider your typical opening day rituals. Do you make sure you are greeting students at the door? Have you prepared your classroom so that it has been customized for them? Do they see their names on their desks? Do you have a birthday wall? Are there organizational systems in the room so that students know where to find materials, submit work, and get help? A distance learning classroom needs precisely the same structures, albeit in a virtual space.

DRAWING ON MY EXPERTISE

What are the five top goals you want to achieve during the first day of school? Don't worry about the environment. Focus on your major goals (e.g., get to know something about each student's interests, establish norms and procedures). You'll refer back to these goals at the end of the module.

1. _____

_____

2. _____

_____

3. _____

_____

4. _____

_____

5. _____

_____

DEVELOP A CLASSROOM MANAGEMENT PLAN FOR DISTANCE LEARNING

A virtual/distance classroom management plan is a teacher-created document that captures the norms, agreements, procedures, and schedules that will be used. Experienced teachers may long ago have internalized their classroom management plan, but a distance learning environment requires some rethinking about what works well for you and your students. Committing a thoughtful and well-constructed plan to paper is a first step in a proactive approach to distance learning and can prevent problems from emerging. It can also be a tool for you to decide in advance of a situation how you will respond. Being proactive, not reactive, is key to good classroom management. Classrooms without a classwide approach to learning have more instances of negative student–teacher interactions and less time spent on academic instruction (Conroy, Sutherland, Snyder, & Marsh, 2008).

It is useful to understand the difference between classroom management and discipline, or behavior management. A classroom management plan outlines the procedures, routines, and expectations for all the students in the class. These include simple routines such as retrieving and replacing materials, as well as more conceptual ideas such as the expectations about the way students interact with others and their learning environment. Discipline, or behavior management, is a component of the overall classroom management plan and is devoted to how problem behavior is prevented, as well as the approach one will use in addressing problem behavior.

Start with a statement of your teaching and learning philosophy. What are your views and beliefs about how teaching and learning should occur in your virtual classroom? What are your beliefs concerning community and diversity? Your statement should be no more than a few sentences long, yet be clear enough for administrators, students, and families to understand your teaching philosophy. Kari Dewall, a sixth-grade teacher, posted her philosophy as a link on her digital classroom wall. Given the limited space, she wrote "I value an environment that allows people to take risks and make mistakes. We are all learning new things and we are here to help each other."

Keep your audiences in mind—if you are teaching very young children, offer an appropriate version for your students. First-grade teacher Tamara Green says, "We need to take care of each other," each time she starts a session with her students. In addition, families who speak a language other than English appreciate your effort to communicate in the home language. If you are not fluent in the home language, seek assistance from your school's parent resource coordinator, parent center, or district language office for translation. This is an investment that is well worth the time.

BEING PROACTIVE, NOT REACTIVE, IS KEY TO GOOD CLASSROOM MANAGEMENT.

Once the classroom management plan has been constructed, you can produce a child-friendly version for students and families. Post this on your learning management system (LMS) and share it digitally with families. This is recommended for two reasons: It serves as an initial means for welcoming students and families at the beginning of the year, and it can become a tool for discussion when a difficulty does arise with a specific student. This module will address many of the aspects of a sound virtual/distance classroom management plan.

NOTE TO SELF

What is your philosophy of teaching and learning in a virtual space? Write no more than 100 words to craft a succinct message.

ESTABLISH NORMS

Groups of people interact according to the norms that have been agreed upon. The interesting thing is that groups will adopt their own norms whether they are formally named or not. You've witnessed this phenomenon countless times when you have met an established group for the first time. You may wonder why that group of old college buddies continuously insults each other or be struck by how solicitous and polite your friend's family gatherings are. Unstated norms in the virtual classroom will evolve, for better or worse.

Norms govern how individuals in the group interact with one another and delineate what will be tolerated and what will not. Note how your interactions change depending on the group you are in. Your behavior is shaped in part by what the group expects of you, whether it is a gathering of neighbors, attendees of a religious organization, or a professional learning community. The norms of the classroom are the beliefs and values you want the collective classroom community to abide by. As any experienced teacher knows, formally stated norms become a handy tool to refer to at the beginning of a class, or when problems arise.

A major learning many experienced in the rapid conversion to distance learning in 2020 is that the norms of the classroom were forgotten. Whether face-to-face instruction proceeded distance learning, or whether you are meeting students for the first time, consider the norms you want your students and yourself to embody. One example of a high school virtual classroom's norms can be found in Figure 2.1. These were developed as a way to establish the norms that govern their peer-to-peer learning.

UNSTATED NORMS IN THE VIRTUAL CLASSROOM WILL EVOLVE, FOR BETTER OR WORSE.

Figure 2.1 Peer-to-Peer Learning Norms
Be open to spend the time it takes to learn.
Be adaptable to your learning and the learning of others.
Create safe space.
Embrace that learning is food for the mind.
Transform learning into action.
Understand that learning is a process that requires patience with self and others.

NOTE TO SELF

What are the norms you want your students to use as they interact with one another and with you in distance learning? We ask some questions to spark your thinking, although not all of them may apply to your classroom.

- What habits and dispositions are needed to be successful learners?

- What should they learn about themselves as learners?

- How should they interact with you and others to maintain learning conditions?

- What should they do with their learning?

LINK NORMS TO CLASS AGREEMENTS

The norms you create for your virtual classroom space become the foundation for the agreements you want to use. These agreements are an essential component for managing a smooth-running learning environment. Well-crafted agreements communicate the teacher's expectations for the class as it relates to climate and student performance. It is important to note that once created, agreements must be explicitly taught to students. Two studies of efficient elementary and middle school classrooms found that in all cases the teachers taught the rules daily during the first week of school using discussion, modeling, and demonstrations (Emmer, Evertson, & Anderson, 1980; Evertson & Emmer, 1982). New technologies further increase the need for rules in digital environments. The use of discussion boards and online collaborative tools has increased the need to ensure that students are taught the norms and expectations of how they work together (Staarman, 2009).

You'll notice that we call them *agreements* rather than *rules*. We do so because agreements represent the social contract of the classroom community, rather than a narrower set of behavioral guidelines that have been written by the teacher alone. A review of fifteen studies on the characteristics of these agreements confirmed what many teachers already know (Alter & Haydon, 2017):

Yamily Sanchez shares her class agreements.

- **A fewer number, rather than more, works better.** The recommendation is about 3 to 5.

- **Co-construct them with students.** That's why we call them agreements. Even young students have a good sense of what is right and fair.

- **State them positively.** Beware of a list of agreements that all begin with the word "No" because these do not tell students what they should do, only what they should not. Behavior cannot exist in a vacuum, and in the absence of clear statements students are left to speculate about what is acceptable.

- **Make them specific in nature.** Agreements that are specific in nature state explicitly what the expected behavior should be, which is a key to building students' ability to self-regulate.

- **Post the agreements.** Once developed, they should be clearly posted in your virtual classroom. One way to do so is to put them on a chart that is behind your head so that students can see them. Another advantage is that you can refer directly to the agreement when redirecting a student's problem behavior. Young children may also benefit from picture symbols to represent each one.

- **Teach and rehearse the expectations.** This is a critical component for ensuring an efficient virtual classroom. The agreements should be taught during each distance learning session during the first week of school and revisited occasionally throughout the remainder of the year, especially after school breaks. The teacher should model each rule so that students can learn what they look and sound like. For example, if one of the agreements is about written communication on discussion boards, model examples of how these are done in ways that are respectful and academically appropriate.

Middle school mathematics teacher Fred Bishop said, "I used to have a list of rules for things kids should not do. Like I had 'Do not talk when I am talking' and 'Do not change seats without permissions' and even 'Do not use pen.' When I went virtual, I took the opportunity to change these. Now the agreements for our class that we talked about together include

- Follow the person who is speaking with your eyes

- Post respectful reactions to ideas in the chat

- Treat members of the class with the care they deserve

These are so much better and they let students know what we expect, as a learning community, of each other."

Agreements serve to convey high expectations, mutual respect, and an acknowledgment of the learning community's needs. A set of rules that are strictly compliance based ("Don't speak unless called on.") tell the students that you're the one with all the power, and they better listen or else. We've actually seen this backfire on several occasions in distance learning classrooms. Teachers who "mute" students for punitive purposes lose them emotionally and psychologically and encounter a lot of difficulty in reengaging at a distance. We've also heard of teachers who get angry with students for using the chat function in their virtual classroom. If you don't want them to use the chat function, then set up your virtual classroom with that feature turned off. It's not fair to get mad at students. Teaching them how to use the chat function in respectful ways is far more useful anyway.

Agreements that emphasize a collaborative spirit ("Listen and respond respectfully, even when you disagree.") signal students that learning is social and done in the company of others. It also lets students know that the role of the teacher is to foster learning, not primarily control and confine students. Classroom agreements are sometimes mistakenly perceived as being necessary only for younger students, but the evidence is to the contrary. A number of studies of adolescents have shown that well-written and enforced agreements contribute positively to teacher–student relationships and increase participation of students in classroom discourse and discussion (e.g., Matsumura, Slater, & Crosson, 2008).

NOTE TO SELF

Revisit the norms you developed in the previous section. What are the three to five agreements you want to co-construct with your students?

1. _____

2. _____

3. _____

4. _____

5. _____

IDENTIFY EXPECTATIONS FOR SYNCHRONOUS DISTANCE LEARNING

Teaching at a distance poses some unique challenges that we never confront in face-to-face teaching. Distance learning is usually a combination of synchronous and asynchronous experiences, and each poses unique challenges. Let's start with synchronous learning. One expectation we had to confront early on when we rapidly switched to virtual learning concerned the issue of cameras. Some students turned them on; most of the adolescents did not. This initially seemed like a no-brainer—of course they should have them on! After all, could you even imagine teaching in a face-to-face class where everyone had a blanket over their heads? To be sure, we rely on being able to read students' facial expressions and body language so that we can teach responsively.

But in talking with teachers and students, we realized the issue of laptop cameras is more complicated. For instance, about 20 percent of our students are Muslim, and girls and women don't wear the hijab in their own homes. In households that are short on space, asking female family members to cover during their children's online learning seems burdensome. There are also students who don't want to show their homes to others for any number of reasons. These are sensitive

Joe Marsella engages preschoolers in a discussion with a puppet.

topics that require sensitive approaches. Here's where we have landed. We ask students to either turn on their camera or use their school picture so that they are easily recognizable to others. And when they are in breakout rooms, most of the students turn their cameras on so that they can see others.

The expectations for synchronous learning vary from one locale to the next and we encourage you to consult with your district's requirements. Some schools that require school uniforms for face-to-face instruction continue to require them during virtual learning. Certainly, it seems that school dress codes should remain in force, in the same way that behavioral ones do. We have also added other possible expectations to use with students when it comes to synchronous learning.

FOR YOUR CONSIDERATION

How will your students learn about your synchronous virtual classroom? Here are some suggested items to address specific questions students are likely to have.

Getting Ready for Your Class Meeting

- Make sure you have completed the pre-class preparation activity so that you'll be ready to learn!
- Think about your goals for learning today. What do you want to achieve?
- Work with your family to find a quiet space that won't disturb other people in your house and won't distract you from learning.
- Prepare your learning space. Make sure you have a clear workspace to write and store your materials.
- If there are items that have personal information you wouldn't want other people to see, move them out of camera range.
- Check your lighting so that your classmates can see you.
- Check to see that your first and last name are on the screen.

During Class Meetings

- Ask clarifying questions so you fully understand the learning intentions and success criteria for the lesson.
- Listen carefully to others and ask good questions!
- Use the reaction buttons to let your classmates know when you agree or disagree and give them a thumbs-up or a round of applause to encourage them.
- The hand raising button helps all of us know when you've got something important to say.
- When you are not speaking, mute your microphone. It helps other people hear.
- Turn off notifications from email and social media so you aren't distracted.
- If you have a smartphone, shut it down so you aren't distracted.

At the Close of the Class Meeting

- Review the goals you set for today. Did you achieve them?
- Ask clarifying questions so you fully understand the learning intentions and success criteria for the lesson. Did you achieve the learning intentions and success criteria? How do you know?
- Make sure you know how to access assigned learning tasks to prepare for the next meeting.

DEVELOP AND TEACH ORGANIZATIONAL AND PROCEDURAL ROUTINES

Another element of your virtual classroom management plan concerns the procedures and organizational structures needed to ensure learning takes place. Although the environment may be different, many of the same organizational requirements remain the same.

1. **Provide weekly and monthly schedules so families and students can organize resources.** Chances are good that there is more than one school-age child in the household. Juggling the online schedules of multiple children can be challenging for even the most organized caregivers. Posting these schedules allows families and students to organize their time.

   - Build weekly and monthly schedules and show students where to find them on your LMS.

   - There may be protocols already developed by your district for designing your website, which is helpful to families as they don't need to learn how four different teachers organize in four idiosyncratic ways.

2. **Furnish a daily schedule at the beginning of the class meeting**. Learning intentions and success criteria are crucial for learning, and we will address those in more detail in Module 6. Providing a schedule for the class meeting assists students in self-regulation of their cognitive and attentional resources.

   - The schedule should list the major learning events of the day in chronological order and may also include times.

   - The consistent use of a posted schedule establishes a predictable learning environment and assists learners in pacing their rate of work.

   - A daily schedule is particularly useful for students who have difficulty transitioning from one task to another and especially for younger children.

   - Posted daily schedules are an excellent support for some students with disabilities who may require more structure.

   - Students who are new to English can benefit from schedules that are paired with pictures.

Thomas Tutogi provides an overview of his weekly schedule.

3. **Teach students the signals you will use.** Teachers need a signal to gain the attention of students at the beginning of class, when students are engaged in dialogue with peers, or when transitioning from one activity to another.

   - The signals should be taught daily during the first week of school and reinforced frequently until students respond quickly and consistently.

   - The use of a signal to gain attention promotes student engagement by minimizing the amount of lost instructional time.

   This point deserves further attention. A study of first-grade classrooms found that teachers who spent time orienting students to the next activity required less time for the transition, and the students in these classrooms spent more time in child-directed learning activities such as collaborative learning than those in classrooms that did not use transition techniques (Cameron, Connor, & Morrison, 2005).

   - Smooth transitions minimize the behavioral difficulties that can arise.

   - Students with behavioral disabilities are especially vulnerable to loosely managed transitions. In many cases, they are blamed for the problem behavior, without consideration for the lack of environmental signals that could have prevented the difficulty from arising in the first place.

   - Students who are new to English are also vulnerable to a lack of signals. When directions are only provided verbally, and are not paired with audible or gestural signals, they may miss the language-based directions and be unfairly viewed as being noncompliant.

   - Use an online elapsed timer display when setting up tasks students will be completing in real time. This further signals to students how to best use their remaining time to complete independent work such as reflective writing.

   - Many virtual classroom platforms feature elapsed timers for small group breakout rooms. Make sure students are aware of these features so that they can monitor their use of time in peer-to-peer small group learning.

4. **Create procedures for how students will retrieve materials.** Few things are more frustrating than trying to figure out where to find materials for online classes.

   - Clearly label digital folders by date and topic so that students can easily locate them.

   - Identify which need to be printed in advance for an online activity. You will want to keep these to an absolute minimum as they can create a burden for families. Having said that, if there is something that students need to print, name it.

5. **Create procedures for how students will submit assignments.** Over the course of the school year, students will turn in a large number of assignments. Invariably, some of these documents will lack important information such as a name or date. Grading is further complicated when the topic of the assignment is unclear. With the advent of digital resources, the naming of documents holds similar problems. It is difficult to process and locate 100 assignments that are all unhelpfully named "Term Paper."

- Teach students a system for heading their assignments at the beginning of the year to make recordkeeping easier.
- Be sure to instruct them on properly naming the file so that you (and they) can locate it quickly. The title of the document should contain the student's last name, the name of the course, and a one- or two-word description.

Heading Requirements	Example	Nonexample
First and last name	Melissa Smith	Melissa S.
Date	4-18-21 or April 18, 2021	April
Subject/Period	US History/3	history
Assignment	p. 87, #1–5	questions

File-Saving Requirements	Example	Nonexample
Last name	Smith	Melissa
Subject/Period	US History 3	history
Assignment	p. 87	questions
Extension	.doc	Left blank

A VIEW FROM THE EARLY YEARS

In order to start the year out on the right foot, planning is key. I've already got ideas, but also questions I need to ask myself to get reading for my primary students. Getting-to-know-you activities will look different in our distance learning environment. My "Meat" and Greet Barbecue might have to be virtual. But I can still send the welcome post card though the US mail and include the family survey and a Me Cube activity in the same envelope. Hopefully every family will send a current photo of their child so I can create the beginning-of-the-year yearbook of photos. That way children can put a name and a face together before our first meeting. I can still spell the names out phonetically, so everyone pronounces our names correctly.

My Broadway Playbill with a picture and paragraph about each child's talents, pets, siblings, and interests can follow later. I hope families will know that when I ask about student interests at the beginning of the school year, they will know that their child's hope to study sprinklers can fit into our Garden Study in May. Will they sign up to bring her sprinkler collection to virtual school?

I can modify my Greeting Apron to include custom greetings to replace the high fives and hugs we can't do right now. I will make my nameplates in several sizes so I can use a mini pocket chart and use them for the Greeting Game from our morning meeting routine. I will create my many lists. Alphabetical lists will help when calling on students in ABC order when I share my screen and project photos of their work and play. The

(Continued)

By Claudia Readwright

(Continued)

chronological list will help when monitoring each child's developmental gains. My gigantic sign that encourages families to participate in our studies can be emailed with a reminder that when I ask for an "expert," it really just means one needs to know more than a five-year-old about the topic!

So many questions to consider as I plan. Will I start at the beginning of the alphabet to assign the Student of the Day? They won't be feeding the fish or watering the class plant. What are their duties? Which of the old ways to group children might I employ? Can I put them in virtual rows on the color carpet? How fluid will the groups be? I will re-create my expectations posters to incorporate our routines in the chat platform (see Figure 2.2).

How will children sit? How will they take turns? What are the voice levels? I will think of ways to limit the number of children present at some meetings and ways to include everyone at others. I will collaborate with my

Figure 2.2 Video Chat Expectations for Younger Students

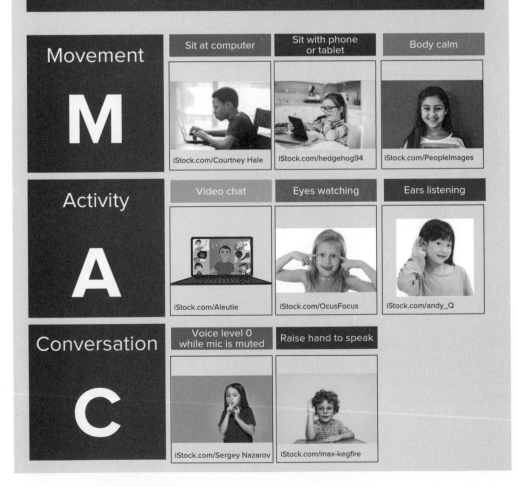

paraprofessional so we can facilitate beak-out rooms. Will I have parents who will want to participate? How will I get them on the same page? Will I have a parent back-to-school forum? Will there be a time most parents can meet? Did our technology roll out during the summer reach all families? Were the hot spots effective so that families would be able to access the free WiFi offered?

I hope children will experience the platform enough that they can decide what makes coming to school a highlight of their day. Then on the anniversary of the signing of the US Constitution on September 17, each child will have their contribution to add to our Class Constitution. I will word each suggestion in a positive way. Rather than "Don't run around," we can say "Sit so everyone can see your face." All who agree will print their name on a piece of paper and say, "yea or nay." I will type it up and email it to families so that each can sign. That way if someone needs a reminder about procedures, routines or expectations, I can refer to the Class Constitution.

And the details! Did I remember to download the elapsed timer? Will my chimes be loud enough to use as my signal? What about the kazoo band? Can we still learn our new melodies before we learn the lyrics? My Bag of Transitions will be at my elbow with the ring of transitions on top. With the *40 Ways to Leave Your Lesson* in my mind and the *I Don't Want to Say Goodbye* song keyed up on my phone, I think I am ready!

DESIGN A CONSIDERATE WEBSITE

Districts routinely use a single platform that all teachers are expected to use. Website design has advanced considerably since the early days of the World Wide Web. Most of us have been on websites that were distracting or unhelpful. This has, in part, led to the requirement that schools and districts include universal design principles to make website usage easier. This has been influenced in part by Section 508 of the Rehabilitation Act of 1998 that requires federal agencies and their affiliates to make websites accessible to people with disabilities. These requirements are beneficial for all users. The Web Content Accessibility Guidelines 2.0 is available at https://www.w3.org/TR/WCAG20/. They recommend that websites be

Tyler Servis gives an overview of his class via a learning management system.

- **Perceivable:** Use color, background, and size of text judiciously to ensure that the information can be viewed.

- **Operable:** Make sure that the information can be driven by the keyboard and that anything timed for display (such as Flash animation) can be adjusted for speed.

- **Understandable:** Use developmentally appropriate text language and avoid placing too much text, or text that is too long, on a single page.

- **Robust:** The information should be useful and compatible with other technologies.

Most LMS platforms have been designed to address many of these issues. Be sure to consult your school or district Instructional Technology coordinator for specific requirements. Consider three distinct places that will be highly useful to students and their families:

THE LANDING PAGE

- The home page should contain the most frequently requested information, including

  - Your contact information (email, mailing address of the school, room number)

  - A description of the course or class and a navigation bar for the other pages.

Also remember

  - While the home page should be visually interesting, it should not be cluttered.

  - Avoid using distracting backgrounds that make it difficult to read.

  - Create a link to your school email address so that students and families can readily contact you.

THE STUDENT PAGE

- This is the ideal place for your syllabus and classroom management plan, as well as a current list of assignments and projects. Nothing looks more dated than a website that features assignments that were due months ago.

- In some cases, you may also post handouts and other materials.

- Consider featuring a reminder for students to contact you with questions and update this information regularly so you can respond in a timely manner.

THE FAMILY PAGE

- The family page should contain information about grading, report cards, and setting up conferences.

- Provide helpful links for families seeking information, such as the school and district websites, content links, and information about your professional training and experiences.

NOTE TO SELF

Students and families retrieve information at any time of the day or week. Develop an FAQ (frequently asked questions) to post on your student and family pages.

QUESTIONS	YOUR RESPONSES
Where can I find weekly and monthly schedules?	
Where do I find assignments and materials?	
How do I submit work?	
How do I retrieve graded work?	
How do I contact the teacher for academic help?	
How do I get technical help?	

Available for download at **resources.corwin.com/distancelearningplaybook**

Aida Rotell discusses her first virtual class and her memory of the first session.

Now, it's time to be a teacher! All of this careful planning is about to pay off. Getting to know your students is the first order of business, whether in a face-to-face or virtual learning environment. Students are also new to each other and need lots of opportunities to learn about one another.

GREET STUDENTS

Could you imagine not greeting the people you live with when they return home for the day? We never think to ourselves "I said hello to my son yesterday, so I really don't need to do it today." Yet in the busy flow of the school year, this is exactly what can happen. We've noticed that is one of the first routines that deteriorates after the first month of school. Even if it is day 179 of a 180-day school year, students deserve to be greeted by name. If it means arriving fifteen minutes earlier to set up your virtual classroom, please do so. Be ready for them as they sign into the class and say hello, use their name, and look them in the eyes.

Some elementary teachers have four or five different no-touch greetings for students (e.g., a wave, a thumbs-up, hand to heart, a *namaste* bow, using the American Sign Language sign for "good morning," the Star Trek finger-spreading sign for "live long and prosper") Let students decide which signal they like to use. It is respectful of the dispositions and cultural norms of students to give them the opportunity to choose their greeting and promotes a sense of autonomy. It's also a great way to get a quick read on a child who might not be ready to learn because of something that happened before she arrived for online learning.

PERSONALIZE THE SPACE

A virtual classroom community is one that shares a common space. Add details so that students see themselves and their unique contributions. You might design your own word cloud of your students' names and use it as your virtual background. Display student work and change it frequently so that they regularly see fresh examples of their efforts on the classroom website. Families will appreciate this, too.

LEARN STUDENTS' NAMES AND HOW TO PRONOUNCE THEM

Addressing people by name is a fundamental signal of respect. When we take the time to learn other people's names, we indicate our interest in them. Hearing

STUDENTS DESERVE TO BE GREETED BY NAME. BE READY FOR THEM AS THEY SIGN INTO THE CLASS AND SAY HELLO, USE THEIR NAME, AND LOOK THEM IN THE EYES.

our own name spoken by another alerts our attention, and creates an emotional link to the person saying our name. A challenge for teachers is in learning the names of their students and pronouncing them correctly. Some names are more familiar than others, depending on the teacher's own experiences. But as anyone who has a difficult name can attest, hearing your name said incorrectly can be discouraging. Creative ways of learning students' names afford opportunities to learn more about their lives and their personalities. Saying a student's name correctly is "a powerful fulcrum for harnessing student engagement and motivation in a classroom" (Elwell & Lopez Elwell, 2020, p. 13). Not knowing or being unwilling to use a student's name contributes negatively to a sense of "otherness" and a belief that he is not valued in the classroom.

Go deeper with students by learning about the story behind their name. We tell stories about how we got our names, which invites a bit of family lore into the classroom and lets students ponder the seemingly impossible notion that once we were babies ourselves. After modeling, we ask students to tell or write about how they got their names. Some may talk about being named after an ancestor or family friend, while others may offer the translated meaning of their name. As they tell the story of their name, we ask them about their preferred names, and if we aren't adept at pronouncing it correctly, we ask them to coach us. Doug asks his students not to let him off the hook and practices each day with them until he is able to say it correctly.

YOUNGER STUDENTS

Teachers of younger students start the school year with songs and chants featuring each child's name to reinforce this information. Yes, you are allowed to sing and clap online! Simple games such as virtual "find someone who" bingo can be completed in breakout rooms. Re-create the rooms every few minutes until all the students in your class have had an opportunity to talk to one another.

OLDER STUDENTS

We have used a silent interview with older students to introduce one another to the class. Students interview one another in pairs by writing questions on a collaborative document. The pairs then answer their partner's questions. After about ten minutes, the students introduce their partner to the rest of the class.

Another technique for older students is to invite them to write a short essay about themselves, including such details as their character traits, aspirations, and biography. Students then convert their essay into a word cloud, choosing fonts, colors, and designs that are pleasing to them. After sharing information about themselves to the class, they can be displayed virtually using the learning management system for the class. Make sure you participate, too, so that your students can learn about you. Encourage students to use these as their virtual backgrounds during the first week of school.

IT IS USEFUL TO PROBE STUDENTS' INTERESTS AT VARIOUS POINTS THROUGHOUT THE YEAR, NOT ONLY DURING THE FIRST WEEK OF SCHOOL.

LEARN STUDENTS' INTERESTS

THERE IS A TREMENDOUS OPPORTUNITY TO FORGE A POSITIVE TEACHER– STUDENT RELATIONSHIP BY TELLING A STUDENT, "I READ THIS AND I THOUGHT OF YOU."

Interest is a key lever for building relevancy into learning, as students with a higher degree of interest in a topic are more likely to perform at higher levels (Palmer, Dixon, & Archer, 2016). Having said that, "interest" isn't likely to manifest itself as a purely academic pursuit. We can't imagine a student breathlessly saying, "I can't wait to learn about the failed Gunpowder Plot of 1604!" But she may be interested in social change, and protests may be a hook for her. She might even be interested in knowing about Guy Fawkes, the leader of the Gunpowder Plot, and the mask that is often worn to disguise the identity of contemporary protesters.

Interest is not static. It is situational and multidimensional across several constructs from low to high. Issues such as its value, frequency, and mastery shift over time, as virtually any teacher can attest. Topics that a student found absorbing at the beginning of the year may suddenly become boring, while a new interest may replace it. Therefore, it is useful to probe students' interests at various points throughout the year, not only during the first week of school.

Successful interest surveys and interviews use language that is developmentally appropriate. For younger students, this may include graphics that allow for ease of response. Older students can complete open-response questions that give them the opportunity to answer in their own words. Many teachers construct their own surveys to tailor them to the class and subject. Your favorite interest surveys are just as valuable in a distance learning environment as they are in a face-to-face classroom.

Before administering the survey, discuss the purpose with your students. Make sure they know that it is not a test and that it is given so that you can be a more responsive teacher for each of them. Even better, take it yourself and share your responses with them so that they can also learn about you. If you decide to do so, tell them about your responses after they have completed their own interest surveys so that you don't influence their answers.

After administering the surveys, construct a chart to note the results. Look for items students have in common with one another. These insights can serve as a means to foster positive peer relationships in the classroom. Use the results to recommend readings and make connections to course content. There is a tremendous opportunity to forge a positive teacher–student relationship by telling a student, "I read this and I thought of you." You can capitalize on student interests by drawing them into topics being taught. For instance, a student who is interested in the night sky might be a useful resource during a unit of study related to astronomy. A student who performs in spoken word events might want to share a related poem with the class. Don't limit connections to academic content. Ask a student who skateboards about the latest trick he is working on. Consult a child who loves video games about recommendations she has for a gift you want to give to a relative in your family. There are many opportunities to capitalize on student interests, but not if you don't know what they are.

NOTE TO SELF

Knowing about your students' interests is a key lever for building relevancy into your curriculum. How will you learn about them? Identify useful interest surveys you might consider using.

CONCLUSION

The first days of virtual instruction, whether they occur at the beginning of the year or intermittently throughout, demand careful attention. If you have the opportunity to initially teach students in a face-to-face classroom, make the most of it by getting them ready for a period of distance learning. Begin by returning to the five goals you identified at the beginning of this module and use them to foreground your developing plans. Make revisions as needed to align your goals with your plans for implementation. As a final task for this module, complete the following self-assessment so that you can identify where to target your efforts.

FACTOR	USING THE "TRAFFIC LIGHT" SCALE, EVALUATE YOUR CURRENT LEVEL OF IMPLEMENTATION (GREEN IS GOOD OR REGULARLY; RED IS THE OPPOSITE).	USING THE SCALE BELOW, DETERMINE HOW IMPORTANT THIS FACTOR IS FOR YOU.
Establishing norms		not at all somewhat very extremely
Linking norms to class agreements		not at all somewhat very extremely
Identifying expectations for synchronous distance learning		not at all somewhat very extremely
Developing and teaching organizational and procedural routines		not at all somewhat very extremely
Designing a considerate website		not at all somewhat very extremely
Greeting students		not at all somewhat very extremely
Learning students' names and how to pronounce them		not at all somewhat very extremely
Learning students' interests		not at all somewhat very extremely

SUCCESS CRITERIA

- I can establish norms for students.

- I can develop class agreements.

- I can identify synchronous distance learning classroom expectations.

- I can teach organizational and procedural routines.

- I can evaluate websites to determine if they are considerate.

- I know my students' names and interests.

TEACHER–STUDENT RELATIONSHIPS FROM A DISTANCE

Ask a teacher what matters in learning and within moments they will be talking about the human connection. Knowing one's students as individuals with rich stories to tell and aspirations for their futures is an essential disposition for teachers. What do you remember about your teachers? Which did you learn best from? Likely it was a teacher with whom you had a positive relationship. Positive relationships between teachers and students form the heart of what Hattie and Zierer (2018) refer to as the mindframes of Visible Learning:

1. I focus on learning and the language of learning.

2. I strive for challenge and not merely "doing your best."

3. I recognize that learning is hard work.

4. I build relationships and trust so that learning can occur in a place where it is safe to make mistakes and learn from others.

5. I engage as much in dialogue as monologue.

6. I inform all about the language of learning.

7. I am a change agent and believe that all students can improve.

8. I give and help students to understand feedback and I interpret and act on feedback given to me.

9. I see assessment as informing my impact and next steps.

10. I collaborate with other teachers.

Consider the extent to which the quality of the relationship between educator and learner underpins many of these mindframes. There is the social sensitivity needed to understand that learning is hard work and to never demean students' efforts. The orientation to dialogic, rather than monologic, teaching suggests that the teacher takes students' ideas seriously and allows them to hear how and what students are thinking or processing. These teachers know that feedback is about what is received, not only what is given, and that a fraught relationship diminishes feedback's usefulness. Teachers hold dear to a core assumption: They deeply believe that they can change the trajectory of a child's educational path and have evidence of their impact to do so.

So, what are the characteristics for a high-quality teacher–student relationship? Before we delve more deeply into that topic, we invite you to reflect on your experiences.

DRAWING ON MY EXPERTISE

What are the three to five quality indicators you use to judge whether a relationship with a student is a positive and productive one?

1. _____

_____

2. _____

_____

3. _____

_____

4. _____

_____

5. _____

_____

CHARACTERISTICS OF TEACHER–STUDENT RELATIONSHIPS

People learn better when they have a positive relationship with the person providing instruction. The evidence of the influence of teacher–student relationships is a positive one, with an effect size of 0.48 (Hattie, 2018). The story behind the data speaks to its potential to accelerate achievement. Elements of teacher–student relationships (Cornelius-White, 2007, p. 113) include

- **Teacher empathy**—understanding
- **Unconditional positive regard**—warmth
- **Genuineness**—the teacher's self-awareness

- **Nondirectivity**—student-initiated and student-regulated activities
- **Encouragement of critical thinking** as opposed to traditional memory emphasis

These student-centered practices are essential in any classroom, perhaps even more so in a virtual one. Establishing these conditions begins from the first interactions students have with the teacher:

- Strong teacher–student relationships rely on effective communication and a willingness to address issues that strain the relationship.

- Positive relationships are fostered and maintained when teachers set fair expectations, involve students in determining aspects of the classroom organization and management, and hold students accountable for the expectations in an equitable way.

- Importantly, relationships are not destroyed when problematic behaviors occur, on the part of either the teacher or students. This is an important point for educators. If we want to ensure students read, write, communicate, and think at high levels, we have to develop positive, trusting relationships with *each* student.

As important, high levels of positive relationships build trust and make your classroom a safe place to explore what students do not know, their errors, and misconceptions. Indeed powerful student–teacher relationships allow errors to be seen as opportunities to learn. A lot of students (and teachers) avoid situations where they are likely to make errors and feel challenged with exposing their lack of knowledge or understanding—but we want to turn these situations into powerful learning opportunities, and this is more likely to occur in high trust environments. And it is not just high positive levels of teacher–student relations, but how you develop high trust student–student relations so one student can talk about their struggles of learning with other students, and the notion of "struggle" becomes a positive and fun activity.

Marco Santiago teaches high school science and has the reputation for being a great teacher. His student believe that they can learn from him and rate him highly. Interestingly students rating of high-quality teaching has a good effect size at 0.45. Students know what good teaching is and are fairly accurate judges of whether or not they can learn from someone. When you ask Marco why his students rate him so highly, he shyly responds,

> Well, I think it's because I get to know them. I work on my relationship with each one of them. But I don't set out to be a friend. I set out to earn their trust so that they will take risks and make mistakes. When that happens, I know that they'll learn more and value the experience. It's been hard in distance learning to do this, but I'm always thinking about how to make sure that students know I care and that they can trust me. So, I start

EVEN IF YOU HAVE HAD PREVIOUS FACE-TO-FACE INTERACTIONS WITH STUDENTS, DON'T NEGLECT REESTABLISHING RELATIONSHIPS WITH YOUR STUDENTS IN A VIRTUAL SPACE.

every session we have with a check-in so that they know that I'm there for them. And I talk about the mistakes I have made teaching online and how exciting it is to learn. They see me as human and are willing to make mistakes so that they can learn too.

Paul Van Straatum talks about how he maintained his relationship with students as he transitioned to distance teaching.

Here's what is important to understand. Even if you have had previous face-to-face interactions with students before, don't neglect reestablishing your relationships with your students in a virtual space. When educators across the world had to rapidly shift from face-to-face to distance instruction in spring 2020, we were reminded of the fragile nature of relationships. Teachers found themselves needing to understand their students in new ways. We were suddenly exposed to our students' worlds as we saw into their homes. Likewise, they saw us in new ways. They study the pictures behind you on your living room wall and see your cat stroll across the screen in the middle of a lesson. Figuring out new parameters of an existing teacher–student relationship can be challenging to navigate. Your students count on you as a constant in their lives.

Dress professionally (you're still a teacher, even when you're teaching from home), show your enthusiasm for them and your work, and make sure that your warmth and regard for them is apparent.

JUDGMENT AND WILL, NOT JUST KNOWLEDGE AND ABILITY

Demetrius Davenport talks about the importance of relationships.

The quality of a teacher–student relationship is dynamic, meaning that it is continually shaped by experiences and context. In the previous module, we shared ideas for ways to initiate relationships with new students, such as using interest surveys, games, and name rituals to learn more about them. Utilizing these approaches is not the same as a relationship with students. These are simply activities that get you through the door with a child or adolescent. The rest is up to you.

Narrow views of the teaching profession focus on knowledge and ability: Does a teacher know how to do _____ and have the ability to implement it? But when it comes to so many aspects of teaching and learning, it is really the teacher's *judgment* and *will* that truly matter (Zierer, Lachner, Tögel, & Weckend, 2018). We separate the "what" of teaching (knowledge and ability) from the "how" (will) and "why" (judgment) about what they do. Teacher–student relationships require not just an investment in fostering new ones ("what"), but in understanding the importance of building and maintaining them ("will") and the social sensitivity to sense when they will best serve the learner ("why").

NOTE TO SELF

How will you establish (or reestablish) relationships with students in a distance learning environment? We've started a list for you. How will you personalize it to your context?

Teacher Empathy How do students seek connections with you?	• Begin synchronous and asynchronous lessons with a positive affirmation (e.g., favorite quotes, a silly joke, short video messages). • Establish virtual office hours for students to drop in for academic support. • Host short check-in conferences with families and the student to see how they are doing and what they need. • •
Unconditional Positive Regard How will your students know you care about them as people?	• Weave into lessons what you have learned about students' pursuits through interest surveys. • Provide polls for students to respond to at the end of class meetings. • Use voice feedback tools on student work so they can hear the sparkle in your voice, rather than read your words without context. • •
Genuineness How will your students know you care about yourself as a professional?	• Dress and groom professionally. • Project a demeanor that is optimistic about them and you. • Make it clear in words and actions that this is a place for learning about themselves, the world, and each other. • •
Nondirectivity How will your students know you hold their abilities in high regard?	• Hold individual conversations with students to help them identify their strengths, goals, and growth areas. • Ask questions that mediate the student's thinking, rather than asking leading questions. • Use shared decision-making about curriculum with students. • •
Encouragement of Critical Thinking	• Foster discussion among peers using questions that open up their thinking. • Every distance learning session includes opportunities for students to write about, illustrate, or discuss their thinking with peers. • Build choice and relevance into assignments and projects. • •

 Available for download at **resources.corwin.com/distancelearningplaybook**

What are your "hows" and "whys" for teacher–student relationships in your practice?

How will you build and maintain relationships throughout the school year in a virtual environment?

Why are relationships central to your distance learning efforts?

PEER-TO-PEER RELATIONSHIPS ARE INFLUENCED, TOO

Teacher–student relationships influence peer perceptions of classmates. When a student asks a question indicating they are lost, do not know where they are going, or are just plain wrong, high levels of peer-to-peer relationships mean that this student is not ridiculed, does not feel that they should be silent and bear their not-knowing alone, and can depend on the teacher and often other students to help them out.

Unfortunately, in some cases, specific students are targeted for behavioral correction while other students engaged in the same behavior are not noticed. We recall a primary grade classroom in which a student was repeatedly chastised for a problematic behavior, but when other children engaged in the same, their behavior was ignored and allowed to continue. And the children noticed. As one of the students said, "Mr. Henderson doesn't want Michael in our class." It's hard to develop positive relationships, and then achieve, when you are not wanted. Being disliked by the teacher or peers has a negative influence on learning, with an effect size of -0.19 (Hattie, 2018). In fact, it is one of the few of 250-plus influences that actually *reverses* learning.

A teacher's dislike for a student is rarely a secret to their classmates. Students are exquisitely attuned to the emotions of the teacher. Think about it: They are observing you closely day after day, and they get very good at being able to read the social environment. They watch how you interact verbally and nonverbally with classmates. You are actually modeling how peers should interact with the specific student. Sadly, students who are disliked by the teacher are more readily rejected by peers than those who are liked by the teacher (Birch & Ladd, 1997). This phenomenon, called *social referencing*, is especially influential among children, who turn to adults to decide what they like and do not like. Elementary students are able to accurately state who is disliked by their teacher. In a study of 1,400 fifth graders, the students reported that they also did not like the children that the teachers told the researchers that they did not like. As the researchers noted, the "targeted" students were held in negative regard six months later, even though they were now in a new grade level with a different teacher (Hendrickx, Mainhard, Oudman, Boor-Klip, & Brekelmans, 2017). Much like a pebble dropped into a pond, being disliked by the teacher ripples across other social relationships and endures well beyond the time span of a negative interaction.

In a distance learning setting, your actions and nonverbal signals are right there for everyone to see and hear. You are on close-up and your reactions are noticeable. Everyone can see when you look away and stop listening to a student. They see when you have muted a classmate's microphone because he was asking questions that took the discussion off topic. Your negative relationship with a particular student can have two possible outcomes. The first is that peers take a dislike to the same student, a phenomenon that is especially

A TEACHER'S DISLIKE FOR A STUDENT IS RARELY A SECRET TO THEIR CLASSMATES.

true in the elementary grades. The second possible outcome is that they take a dislike to you. And a student who doesn't like you makes your job much more difficult. It is far more challenging to learn from someone you don't like (Consalvo & Maloch, 2015).

Brian Leach spotlights two students in each session. He wants to ensure that he is demonstrating that he values each of his learners and provides them his full attention, and that of the class, during the spotlight. As Mr. Leach says, "I am super careful about my body language all the time, but when I do a spotlight, I show the student that I am very interested. And really, I am. They know in advance but I don't tell the rest of the class. And they share interesting things. Then we do a question and answer period and it's great for oral language development. But it started so that I could show students that I was interested in them as people."

REFLECTIVE WRITING

This is just for you. Who are the students at risk in your distance learning classroom? Use initials only. What barriers are you currently experiencing?

A "CHILLY" CLASSROOM

Uriel Cortez talks about his experience as a student and how warm teachers changed him.

Some students keep us a bit more at arm's length. They may be reserved in nature, or distrustful of teachers in general. Others exhibit problematic behaviors that disrupt the learning environment. In some cases, we just don't like a particular kid. He just rubs you the wrong way and you're not even sure why. Unfortunately, the students we don't like, especially those we perceive as being low achieving, pay for it in terms of positive teacher attention. A study of differential teacher treatment of students (Good, 1987) found that low-achieving students

- Are criticized more often for failure

- Are praised less frequently

- Receive less feedback

- Are called on less often

- Have less eye contact from the teacher

- Have fewer friendly interactions with the teacher

- Experience acceptance of their ideas less often

Each of these can just as easily occur in a virtual classroom. There is another term for this: a *chilly classroom climate* in which some students do not feel they are valued and instead feel that "their presence . . . is at best peripheral, and at worst an unwelcome intrusion" (Hall & Sandler, 1982, p. 3). We do not in any way believe that these differential teacher behaviors are conscious and intentional. One speculation is that because educators don't feel successful with students they view as lower achieving, we subconsciously avoid contact with them. After all, we were human beings long before we became educators, and as social animals we attempt to surround ourselves with people who make us feel good about ourselves. Students who are not making gains make us feel like failures, and so we detach ourselves even more.

Now view Good's list from the opposite direction—students we see as being high achieving get more of us. Our attention, our contact, our interactions are more frequent, sustained, and growth producing. It is understandable that we gravitate to those students that make us feel successful as educators. But it is also a version of the Matthew effect, this time in attention rather than reading—the rich get richer while the poor get poorer (Stanovich, 1986). In this case, it's our positive attention that is gold.

By Claudia Readwright

A VIEW FROM THE EARLY YEARS

The relationship between a teacher and student is the bedrock for the child's relationship with school. There are so many things we can do to make our relationships stronger. Since a child's name is the greatest connection to their identity and individuality, learning and using their names is super important. Calling someone by their name connects us and increases communication, trust, empathy, and accountability. We greet children and families at arrival and use their names in our greetings. Terms of endearment like *sweetie* or *honey* cannot replace the importance of using their names. Have a collection of name songs and sing them all day long. As children arrive into your chat platform, call out to them. "Look, children . . . Nancy is here! (Tune: "Farmer in the Dell") 'Nancy is here. She gives us joy and cheer. Sure, it's true, we say to you, we're glad to see you here.'" Name rituals, such as origin or meaning, are fun as extensions to books like *Chrysanthemum*. Counting the letters in names and comparing them to Chrysanthemum's is a hit. Early learners never tire of using body percussion in connection to their names. There are Pinterest boards dedicated just to names!

Establishing a relationship with our students' families is also very important. The isolation from sheltering can be eased by providing adult times to chat. We open an Online Chat as our office hours. It gives parents a chance to connect and offer support to one another. They can arrange for a private miniconference during those times. Offering alternative times to families who cannot make morning online chats goes a long way to building relationships.

When we think about how to increase our positive attention, we can circle back to what we know about using children's names and calling on children. We like to call on *nonvolunteers*. There are many ways this can be done, using cards, dice, random word generator, craft sticks, alphabetical lists, for example. Let's remember that volunteers *do* serve a purpose in our classrooms. The rule of thumb is calling on three nonvolunteers before calling on a volunteer. After 3 correct responses from the nonvolunteers, volunteers can be called on to enrich the answers or pose an alternative idea. Another strategy is to pull a name stick and call on that child then call on their chat partner. If you have assigned colors to groups of children, you could call on children in the same color row. Our goal is to ensure the number and quality of interactions with each student is intentionally monitored.

In order to make sure every live session includes discussion opportunities, planning and communication are requisites. We provide a lesson menu which contains a question of the day. It is used for shared discussion and writing. In distance learning, parents are leading the discussion, writing what the child dictates and sending us the photo of the writing. We check what's been shared and continue with follow up questions in our online chats. Before signing off, we frontload what's coming up and to start thinking about a future topic.

REACHING THE HARD TO TEACH

Imagine flipping the switch on this narrative by intentionally increasing your positive attention efforts with students you have identified as being difficult to reach. We don't mean suddenly focusing all your attention on the three students that fall into that category while neglecting all the others. A quick pivot like that might be viewed as alarming or dismaying. However, waging a thoughtful campaign to change the dynamic is likely to have another benefit. Those students are likely to grow on you. We'll borrow advice attributed to Archbishop Desmond Tutu that sometimes you have to "act your way into being." In other words, sometimes the change in behavior precedes the change in perception.

SOMETIMES YOU HAVE TO "ACT YOUR WAY INTO BEING."

Many of these behaviors seem to come naturally, at least when it comes to those students with whom we have a positive relationship. But it takes deliberate action to disrupt established communication patterns that are avoidant in nature. Identify the two or three students you want to target for increased positive attention. During live interactions, keep a tally for yourself about the following teacher-initiated behaviors.

INTERACTION	STUDENT 1	STUDENT 2	STUDENT 3
Did I greet the student by name when they entered the virtual classroom?			
How many times did I use their name (not as a correction) during the session?			
Did I ask them a critical thinking question related to the content?			
Did I ask them a personal question?			
Did I pay them a compliment?			
How many times did I provide them with praise for learning performance?			

online resources Available for download at **resources.corwin.com/distancelearningplaybook**

Keelie Bauman shares her ideas for reaching hard-to-teach students.

After you have collected data on yourself across several sessions, examine it and make some decisions about what you need to do more of and less of. In addition, reflect on any changes you have perceived in their reactions to you. It isn't always comfortable to look at these kinds of data, but it is something that courageous educators do because it fuels their own improvement. We'll harken back to the beginning of this module and the mindframes of great teachers: *I see assessment as informing my impact and next steps.*

REFLECTIVE WRITING

What am I noticing in the data I have collected? What changes have I noticed in these students?

Patterns and trends in the data	
Changes in identified students	
Actions and next steps	

 Available for download at **resources.corwin.com/distancelearningplaybook**

INCREASE YOUR TOUCHPOINTS WITH ALL STUDENTS

Disney entertainment parks strive to provide every visitor with what they call a "world class experience." One focus of their efforts is the concept of touchpoints, which they define as ranging from personal interactions to the functional items such as the signage in their parking lots. There are parallels to the work that we do in distance learning environments. Our touchpoints include the interactions we have with students, but also extend to the website we use on the learning management system, the contacts we make with families, and the directions we provide for asynchronous learning.

Given the increased challenge that distance learning poses, it is crucial that you develop tools and systems so that you can actively monitor the number and quality of touchpoint interactions with each student on your roster. Most distance learning schedules have far fewer number of hours of contact than in face-to-face instruction. Casual conversations in the hallway or the cafeteria aren't possible, and too often a misplaced focus on doing as much direct instruction as possible in live sessions has meant that interaction opportunities have decreased even more. Use these approaches to maximize ways to build and maintain relationships across the school year:

1. **Have a system for calling on students and noticing who hasn't participated**. Teachers call on students to respond to questions and to participate in learning tasks. However, the pattern of who is called upon is often uneven and may leave some students out of the discussion. For example, one study of questioning in elementary and middle school classrooms found that boys were called on more frequently than girls because they volunteered more often (Altermatt, Jovanovic, & Perry, 1998).

   An effective way to overcome the limitations of calling on students disproportionately is to use a method for randomly calling on students. This allows several goals to be achieved simultaneously. The most obvious is that it decreases the likelihood that some students will be overlooked. Many secondary students have perfected the ability to remain unnoticed in virtual classrooms, sitting quietly on the fringes of the discussion. While the goal of a random questioning method is not to put students on the spot, it is to encourage other voices in the classroom discourse. In addition, it gives the teacher a richer and more nuanced portrait of the level of understanding the class possesses at a moment in time. If the only students that are called on are the ones who know the answer (and are therefore more likely to volunteer), then the teacher is not aware of what may need to be retaught, and to whom. Don't use a random question method as a way to catch students off-guard. Always announce the student's name and make sure you have their attention before posing the question. This is respectful and contributes positively to the relationship between the you and the student.

IT ISN'T ALWAYS COMFORTABLE TO LOOK AT THESE KINDS OF DATA, BUT IT IS SOMETHING THAT COURAGEOUS EDUCATORS DO BECAUSE IT FUELS THEIR OWN IMPROVEMENT.

- **Craft sticks.** Write student names on wooden craft sticks and place in a can. Draw names to respond and set aside those that have been used. You can even label one (or more) of the sticks "teacher's choice" and call on students that you want to when you draw that stick.

- **Name cards on a ring**. Write names on index cards and punch a hole in the top left corner and place them a two-inch binder.

- **Pass it on.** After responding, allow the student to choose the next person. Be careful that this does not become a popularity contest.

- **Keep a tally on your class roster.** Simple tick marks let you know who has been talking and who hasn't.

2. **Make sure every live session includes whole group and small group discussions**.

   Without discussion opportunities, you have very few ways to use your students' names, ask nondirective and critical thinking questions, and demonstrate your unconditional regard for them. If allowed in your school system, use the "breakout room" feature to provide students opportunities to engage in dialogue with small groups of peers.

   - **Curtail your lecture time** by recording asynchronous experiences and increase the opportunities for discussion when you are together.

   - **Older students can be assigned to develop questions** for use in discussions of readings that were completed asynchronously. The discussion director writes two or three discussion questions in advance of the session and shares them with the teacher. This achieves several goals, including expanding choice in the curriculum and conveying your respect for them as thinkers.

3. **If you assign discussion boards, actively participate in them**. Some distance learning classes use discussion boards for students to respond to a prompt and to one another. Few things are more discouraging, however, than wondering if the teacher even reads them, or just assigns a numerical score.

   - Be an active presence on your discussion boards by replying regularly to student postings. You don't have to respond to all of them, but students should see your name regularly.

   - Keep track of who you respond to so that you can be sure to distribute your attention equitably.

4. **Use "pop-up pedagogy" to increase touchpoints across the week.** Your live virtual sessions are limited, but students should still be engaging with your content throughout the week. Increase the number of touchpoints outside of live virtual sessions using an approach Fitzpatrick (2016) calls *pop-up pedagogy*. You know those ads that fly up onto your screen when you're looking at a website? Those are pop-ups. And while we don't mean that you literally are placing ads, think of pop-ups as ways for students

Alex Gonzalez shares his thinking about the value of discussions in distance learning.

to think about your class even when you're not in front of them. Here are some ideas:

- If your school has a two-way communication system such as Remind, send messages to students and their families several times a week.
  - A greeting with a motivational quote can be effective (e.g., "The expert in anything was once a beginner. Congratulations on improving your expertise in binomial equations!")
  - An intriguing question can be used to foreshadow upcoming content (e.g., "Have you wondered why your cell phone battery dies? We'll be discussing this in physical science on Thursday. Bring your ideas!")
- Post photos of students and their assignments on your learning management system. If your website includes a carousel feature, add them to the top of your website so they see themselves and each other each time they log on.
- Ask younger students to submit photos of themselves at home with their completed assignment. As one example, a physical education teacher made a short video of the directions for making a pillow fort and sent it to the kindergartners. They had a family member take a picture of their completed effort and send it back to him. He then featured his students' efforts on a collaborative document so that all the students could see each other's creations.
- Craft an email newsletter each week to families explaining what their children did in the past week and what they will be studying in the coming week. You don't need to make this fancy or extensive. These newsletters can also be posted on your website, but many families will miss it unless they go to the website. Sending emails means that more families are likely to encounter the information. Be sure to use your district's translation software so that households with other heritage languages have equal access.
- Personalize directions for assignments by making a short video rather than only providing written directions. When you think about it, you rarely read written directions verbatim to a face to face class. Instead, you augment the written directions with your own verbal language. Let them see and hear you, not just read what you've written.
- Use voice recording feedback tools on students' assignments. Not only is this faster than typing out written feedback, it's much easier to personalize it. Be sure to say the student's name, provide feedback about strengths and suggestions for next steps, and pose a thought-provoking question to keep the conversation going.

Brianna Castellanos talks about her pop-up pedagogy.

Of course, this is by no means an exhaustive list, and you probably have other ideas you are already using, or that you have heard colleagues discuss. Our intention is to spark your creative thinking for how to build and maintain teacher–student relationships across the school week.

NOTE TO SELF

How will you increase touchpoints for all your students?

How will you call on students?	
How will you notice who hasn't participated so you can re-engage them?	
What will you need to be mindful of to create more discussion opportunities during live virtual sessions?	
How will you be a presence on your discussion boards?	
What is your "pop up pedagogy" plan to stay connected with students when you are not in a live session?	
What is your "pop-up pedagogy" plan to stay connected with families?	

 Available for download at **resources.corwin.com/distancelearningplaybook**

CONCLUSION

Quality teacher–student relationships are foundational to learning environments but can be more challenging in a distance learning one. Revisit the three to five quality indicators you recorded at the beginning of this module. Are there any you would change based on new learning? As a final task for this module, complete the following self-assessment so that you can identify where to target your efforts.

FACTOR	USING THE "TRAFFIC LIGHT" SCALE, EVALUATE YOUR CURRENT LEVEL OF IMPLEMENTATION (GREEN IS GOOD OR REGULARLY; RED IS THE OPPOSITE).	USING THE SCALE BELOW, DETERMINE HOW IMPORTANT THIS FACTOR IS FOR YOU.
Reflecting on teacher–student relationships and mindframes of great teachers		not at all · somewhat · very · extremely
Considering characteristics of teacher–student relationships		not at all · somewhat · very · extremely
Maintaining teacher–student relationships		not at all · somewhat · very · extremely
Fostering healthy peer relationships		not at all · somewhat · very · extremely
Reaching the hard-to-teach student		not at all · somewhat · very · extremely
Increasing touchpoints with students and families		not at all · somewhat · very · extremely

SUCCESS CRITERIA

- I can describe the characteristics of valuable teacher–student relationships.

- I can use the elements of teacher–student relationships (teacher empathy, unconditional positive regard, genuineness, nondirectivity, and encouragement of critical thinking) in my interactions with students.

- I leverage my relationships to create an environment in which errors are valued.

- I recognize the signs of a chilly classroom and work to avoid that feeling.

- I redouble my efforts to reach hard-to-teach students.

- I can design systems that increase touchpoints for students virtually.

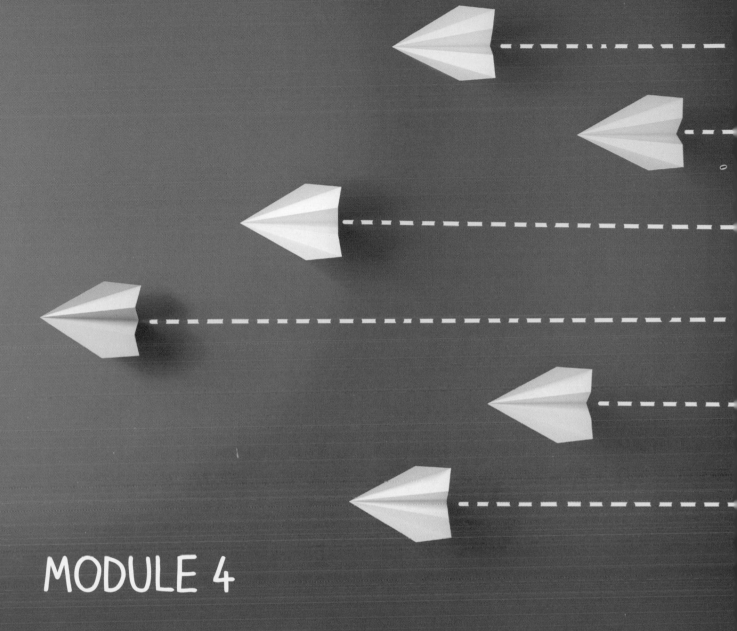

MODULE 4

TEACHER CREDIBILITY AT A DISTANCE

- I am learning
  what teacher
  credibility
  means.

- I am learning
  ways to
  maintain my
  credibility with
  students from
  a distance.

IMPORTANTLY,
THE CREDIBILITY
A TEACHER HAS
WITH THEIR
STUDENTS
CHANGES;
IT'S DYNAMIC.
IT'S NOT THE
SAME FOR ALL
STUDENTS
AT THE
SAME TIME.

Do your students believe that they can learn from you? If your answer is yes, they will likely learn a lot more. In fact, the effect size of teacher credibility, which is the label we give to the concept that students believe that they can learn from their teachers, is 1.09. WOW! Right? It's powerful. But, like all of the influences that are likely to significantly accelerate learning, it's hard to accomplish. Importantly, the credibility a teacher has with their students changes; it's dynamic. It's not the same for all students at the same time. In the last module, we talked about teacher–student relationships, which are important. Teachers and students should have healthy, growth-producing relationships, in part because students learn more when these are present. It's hard to imagine that a teacher could be credible with students without a strong relationship. But teacher credibility extends to other areas, specifically trust, competence, dynamism or passion, and immediacy or perceived closeness.

Before we ask you to draw on your expertise, let's visit a virtual class meeting and see what we notice about credibility. The students in Matt Anders's algebra class had a test. They had been learning about solving first degree equations. Two days before the test, Mr. Anders provided his students with a practice version. They could take this practice version as many times as they wanted but they had to identify areas in which they needed more practice or additional learning. As Mr. Anders said on the video that introduced the practice test, "Greetings Algebrains! You have worked hard with me on these and I hope you'll trust me and yourselves to complete the practice versions on your own. That way, you'll know what you know and where you still need learning. I'll be online for three hours and you can pop in and share your screen any time that you want. We can work together on any of the sample items that give you trouble. I know you know this material. I'm not here to trick you. Your assessment will look a lot like the practice version, but with different numbers and variables. Remember, it's your math and you can do this."

When the students clicked on the icon to take the test, the first thing that popped up was a hint, which read "Remember, we need to isolate variables on one side. Oh, but you already knew that." The students were presented with a problem to solve. Mr. Anders had randomized the problems and answers, which his students were accustomed to.

Amelia's first problem was $3x - 5 = 19$. Before answering, she sent a message to her teacher asking, "It doesn't matter which side the variable is on, right?" Almost instantly, he responded, "Nope, as long as the variable is isolated. Message me if you want to talk further. Or tell me the problem and what you're going to select so we can chat."

Amelia replied, "Thanks. Actually, I just wanted to check that you were there. I knew that."

Mr. Anders replied, "Got me. But I am here, really."

It may be easier to see teacher credibility in a physical classroom, but we hope you noticed several things about this small slice of Mr. Anders's teaching. He is trustworthy. His students know what to expect from him and he does not try to trick them. He seems competent, but we would probably know more about his students' perceptions of his competence if we could see one of the lessons in which he demonstrates his thinking or coaches their learning. In terms of passion, the video seemed as if he were coming through the screen. He was dressed for success, animated, and excited. And finally, even though they were apart, students knew that they could reach him and that he was there.

DRAWING ON MY EXPERTISE

Consider the following questions about your past experiences with teacher credibility.

1. How have I established trust with my students?

2. How do I demonstrate competence to my students?

3. How do I display my dynamism to my students?

4. How do I ensure that my students feel close to me?

Let's explore teacher credibility further and then identify ways to develop and maintain your credibility from a distance.

TEACHER CREDIBILITY DEFINED

At the basic level, teachers need to be seen as believable, convincing, and capable of persuading students that they can be successful. Students know which teachers can make a difference. As we have previously noted, "The dynamic of teacher credibility is **always** at play" (Fisher, Frey, & Hattie, 2016, p. 10). Thankfully, there are specific actions that teachers can take to increase their credibility in each of the following four areas (Fisher, Frey, & Smith, 2020).

TRUST

Students need to know that their teachers really care about them as individuals and have their best academic and social interests at heart. Students also want to know that their teachers are true to their word and are reliable. Here are a few points about trust:

1. If you make a promise, work to keep it (or explain why you could not).

2. Tell students the truth about their performance (they know when their work is below standard and wonder why you are telling them otherwise).

3. Don't spend all of your time trying to catch students in the wrong (and yet be honest about the impact that their behavior has on you as an individual).

4. Examine any negative feelings you have about specific students (they sense it and it compromises the trust within the virtual classroom).

As Covey (2008) noted in *The Speed of Trust*, when it exists, things go faster. These more generic recommendations will continue to serve us well in a distance learning format. But there are additional considerations. In fact, Hoy and Tschannen-Moran identified five elements for trust to be developed and maintained:

- **Benevolence:** Confidence that one's well-being or something one cares about will be protected by the trusted party . . . the assurance that others will not exploit one's vulnerability or take advantage even when the opportunity is available.

- **Honesty:** The trusted person's character, integrity, and authenticity . . . acceptance of responsibility for one's actions and not distorting the truth in order to shift blame to another.

IT MAY SEEM SIMPLE, BUT WE HAVE WITNESSED A DECREASE IN THE TRUST STUDENTS HAVE IN THEIR TEACHERS WHEN THEY SEE THEIR TEACHERS AS UNRELIABLE.

- **Openness:** The extent to which relevant information is shared . . . openness signals reciprocal trust.

- **Reliability:** Consistency of behavior and knowing what to expect from others . . . a sense of confidence that one's needs will be met in positive ways.

- **Competency:** The ability to perform as expected and according to standards appropriate to the task at hand. (von Frank, 2010, p. 2)

Maggie Fallon talks about how she maintains trust.

As teacher Brianna Salazar noted, "Students ask me questions and expect an honest answer. It's the same whether we are face-to-face or online. But I noticed that when they are at home, sometimes they ask me questions that wouldn't really be asked in school. I need to answer, but also remember that I'm still their teacher."

We have found that teachers are being asked a number of questions that have them searching for appropriate answers. The lack of physical proximity and the fact that they are home seems to invite questions that might not have been asked at school. Our advice is that you answer honestly when you can and that you are clear about the reasons when there are questions you cannot answer. For example, first-grade teacher Ari Brown was asked by one of her students if her grandmother was going to die from the virus. Immediately another student asked if Ms. Brown was going to die. Depending on the age of the student, you might respond that no one knows for sure who gets sick and the doctors and scientists are working really hard to find solutions. High school English teacher Seth McGuire was asked who he would vote for in the upcoming presidential election. Mr. McGuire answered that he was not sure yet but that voting in the United States was a very private matter and not usually discussed. As he said, "We have private places to vote in the US called polls so that people can vote what is in their heart."

It may seem simple, but we have witnessed a decrease in the trust students have in their teachers when they see their teachers as unreliable. And it's as simple as being late for an online learning session. As Leo said about his fourth-grade teacher, "She doesn't really start on time. She's late a lot. And she gets frustrated and ends the meeting before we're supposed to be finished. Then I get in trouble with my dad because I'm supposed to be in class."

Mikayla, a ninth grader, also noted that her teacher compromised their trust. In this case, it was based on the feedback that was promised but never received. As Mikayla said, "On our discussion boards, she gives everybody 10. It doesn't matter if we write really interesting things or not. We just all get 10. It's like she doesn't care. The quizzes are graded by the computer and I don't even think she knows our scores. And when we submit assignments, the comments are just like 'good work' or 'I see your point' or 'that's interesting.' It doesn't help you get any better." As Mikayla noted, lack of honest feedback broke the trust she had with the teacher.

On a more positive note, Abdul said that his world history teacher records audio files and talks about his student's work. As Abdul said, "We get a personal commentary back on our work. He talks directly to us, each person, and tells us what he is thinking when he looks at what we did. He talks about things that are effective and accurate and things that are confusing or where we made mistakes. And he tells us what the next step is. I like it when he says, like, 'So Abdul, your political cartoon was spot on for the issue. And your use of exaggeration really caught my attention. But I think it might be a little too obvious. I think you might want to be more subtle so the person looking at is has to do some thinking. Do you want to talk further about the art of being subtle?' That really got me and so I scheduled a time to talk with him to learn more. I know he's gonna be honest and that it will make me better."

**By Claudia
Readwright**

A VIEW FROM THE EARLY YEARS

We are asked to draw on our expertise to determine how we can strengthen our credibility with students. There is a close relationship between truth and trust, and young learners trust that their teacher is truthful. In a distance learning world, that means showing up on time, looking like the teacher they remember from class, and displaying our positive spirit. When we ask children to make something and bring it to our chat to showcase their learning, we need to give them time to share. If we ask for a photo ahead of time, we can honor their work in a slide show that allows them to describe their project. Afterward, we will want to give effective feedback. Probing questions that lead them to their next steps are within our early learner's scope. There are ways to strengthen our expertise in order to be the competent teacher every child deserves. Do your homework when it comes to your study. If you ask a question of the day, have the answer and a photo ready that offers a visual representation of the answer. Appear calm, confident, and aware of your body language.

Being passionate about our work includes being enthusiastic about our learning. In our physical classroom, you might find a round table near our front door. An interesting or unusual object is on the round table. Children quickly stow their belongings away to inspect the object. They gather to make predictions about the item, how it might be used, and how it is related to our topic or study. Children draw the item in their Wonder Journal and label or write their thoughts. At our signal, we gather to share our work. In our virtual classroom, the screen can be shared to show an item and the same routine can be followed. If there is a *Wonderopolis* page that fits our topic, that could replace the object activity. The journal experience would remain the same. Sharing a story about the item can be exciting, relevant, and a universal human experience.

Most young children like having us close. They'd love our lap to be their spot. Sitting next to us in the circle would make their day. They seek our eye contact. They call out, "Look at me!" more times than we can count. How we make ourselves accessible in our virtual classroom takes some creative thinking. Appointing a Student of the Day, Teacher Helper, or Ambassador gives that child roles of leadership and gives them an opportunity to shine. Remembering to use each child's name assures them that they are important and that you see them.

Leading an interactive class involves being organized and prepared. Young learners like familiar routines. They appreciate when we follow a predictable schedule. We send out our weekly lesson menu by Sunday so families know what to expect in the coming week. As they enter the room, we sing a welcome or hello song using their names. When most have arrived, we can put on our cardigans or beginning-of-class cue and start our session. Then we can announce our learning intention for the day. "Today we will do three things. We will meet Vincent van Gogh, study his sunflower print, and draw real sunflowers."

NOTE TO SELF

Based on the descriptions of trust, what ideas do you have for maintaining and enhancing this aspect of credibility at a distance?

COMPETENCE

In addition to trust, students want to know that their teachers know their stuff and know how to teach that stuff. They expect an appropriate level of expertise and accuracy from their teachers. Further, students measure competence by the ability of the teacher to deliver instruction that is coherent and organized. They expect that lessons are well paced and the information is accurate.

1. Make sure you know the content well and be honest when a question arises that you are not sure about (this requires planning in advance).

2. Organize lesson delivery in a cohesive and coherent way.

3. Consider your nonverbal behaviors that communicate competence, such as the position of your hands when you talk with students or the facial expressions you make (students notice defensive positions, and nonverbal indications that they are not valued when they speak).

THE TASK IS THE SAME, BUT HOW YOU VIEW IT CAN INFLUENCE YOUR EFFORTS, THE STRESS YOU EXPERIENCE, AND THE SATISFACTION YOU RECEIVE.

We have several modules later in this playbook devoted to developing and enhancing our collective competence in distance learning. If distance learning is new for you, you'll probably feel like a beginning teacher again. You can choose to think of this as a wonderful learning opportunity or a royal pain. The task is the same, but how you view it can influence your efforts, the stress you experience, and the satisfaction you receive.

As we discuss further in Module 6, Engaging Tasks, it's impossible to keep up with all the distance learning tools available. We have found solace in knowing that the functions have remained essentially the same, even though the tools change regularly. Consider the need to search for information. Some of us remember traveling to the library and looking up information in the card catalog and then going to find the book on a shelf someplace. We have not stopped searching for information, but the tools we use to find that information have changed (and they'll continue to change throughout our lifetimes). We cannot be competent, or even knowledgeable, about every tool out there. But we can learn some new tools that serve the functions we need to accomplish.

When Susan Hargrove first engaged in teaching from a distance, she was nervous. She was worried that she would "do it wrong" and "make a fool of herself" in front of her students. Her first live session via computer video was not great but she told her students that she was learning and how excited she was. As she said, "So, this is my first time doing this. I am a little nervous but I'm also excited. At the end, I want to ask for feedback. I want to be sure that you're learning and I'm willing to make adjustments so that you can learn from me and each other." At the end of her first session, when she invited students to provide feedback, they were uniformly kind and offered a number of ideas for her to consider. For example, Bradley suggested that she use the reaction buttons. Maria hoped that she would annotate on the screen so that they could track where she was. And Tonja requested that they get to keep the same breakout groups during the session so that they could keep adding to their discussions. Relieved that it went well, Ms. Hargrove called her principal and excitedly reported, "I think that they actually learned something from me today. And I learned more about what they want from me. It feels really good and their ideas are great. I'm going to contact the technology office right now so that I can practice these ideas before class tomorrow."

Interestingly, when teachers change their instructional strategies too frequently, students believe that they are not competent. As one student said, "I'm not sure she knows what she is doing because she tries something different every time." To build on our competency, learning routines should be predictable and understandable to students. That's not to say that change is forbidden. But rather that you plan some tasks that students come to expect. Some variety is good, but so is consistency.

SOME VARIETY IS GOOD, BUT SO IS CONSISTENCY.

Middle school science teacher Arnold Anaya sums it up this way: "I flow each week so that students know what to expect. Generally, the same flow each week. Of course, the content changes and I might add a few tasks here and there, but my students know what to expect from this class. For example, they know on Mondays they're going to see me on video. I've recorded a lot of information in short bits for them and I've embedded quizzes into the videos. They can do these over and over to get them all right. There's no penalty for practice. On Tuesdays, they know that we're going to have a reading. I read live with them, modeling my thinking and asking questions in the chat. I offer this several times each Tuesday and they can attend any session that they want. I know that sounds strange to some people, but my students like choices. On Tuesday, they also know that they will receive the science connection. It's an assignment that requires them to find current information that relates to the topic we're studying that week. They have until Friday to submit and it's based on some of the background knowledge we built on Monday. On Wednesday and Thursday, they have collaborative tasks and virtual labs. These change, but they know that collaboration and experiments are Wednesday and Thursday. I also offer tutorials several times per day on Wednesday and Thursday. I require some students to attend and make them optional for others. If the initial assessment information tells me that a student needs more time and attention in a particular unit, I schedule them for sessions. In addition, I schedule all of the students with disabilities in these sessions for the added time. Our special educator joins me for those meetings to provide additional support. On Fridays, we have quizzes and writing tasks. They can take the quizzes over as many times as they want, provided that they explain why an answer was incorrect. When they do, I clear the attempt and they take it again. I think that this predictability really helps them navigate the content. In fact, I think they pay more attention to the content because they know what is expected of them."

Javier Vaca talks about ways to maintain competence.

Based on the descriptions of competence, what ideas do you have for maintaining and enhancing this aspect of credibility at a distance?

DYNAMISM

Joanna Schaefer talks about dynamism and passion.

This dimension of teacher credibility focuses on the passion teachers bring to the classroom and their content. It is really about your ability to communicate enthusiasm for your subject and your students. And it's about developing spirited lessons that capture students' interest. To improve dynamism,

1. **Rekindle your passion for the content you teach** by focusing on the aspects that got you excited as a student. Remember why you wanted to be a teacher and the content you wanted to introduce to your students. Students notice when their teachers are bored by the content and when their teachers aren't really interested in the topic. We think that a teacher's motto should be "Make content interesting!"

2. **Consider the relevance of your lessons.** Does the content lend itself to application outside the classroom? Do students have opportunities to learn about themselves and their problem solving? Does the content help them

become civic minded and engaged in the community? Does it connect to universal human experiences, or ask students to grapple with ethical concerns? When there isn't relevance, students check out and may be compliant learners rather than committed learners.

3. **Seek feedback from trusted colleagues about your lesson delivery.** Ask peers to sit in on a virtual lesson to focus on the energy you bring and the impact on students' demeanors, rather than the individual instructional strategies you use. Students respond to the passion and energy in a lesson, even if they didn't initially think they would be interested.

Wangberg (1996) argues that there are at least four ways to demonstrate passion in the classroom. He notes that "the best teachers are people who are passionate about their subject *and* passionate about sharing that subject with others" (p. 199).

Your passion did not change because you are teaching from a distance. Make sure that your students know that. We're almost embarrassed to say this, but your dynamism shows in what you wear to class. Consider this: If you wouldn't wear it to the building, don't wear it on camera with your students. Students expect their teachers to look a certain way. We are not suggesting that you must wear a tie or business clothes. We are saying that how you look matters and failure to consider this can compromise your credibility. As one student said, "I think she forgot we had class. She looked like she just got out of bed and didn't even comb her hair." That's not good.

But dynamism is more than an outward appearance. It's also about the excitement you bring to the sessions, both synchronous and asynchronous. There are a number of ways to demonstrate enthusiasm, including the tone in your voice, the emotional stories you tell, or the presentation techniques you use. Regardless of the approach, students should know that you care about the content.

Students judge our dynamism based on the instructional materials that we use. Old, wordy slides are deadly. Extra slides cost nothing so please do not crowd all of the information on a single slide. Space it out. Use visuals. Change fonts and text size. Add multimedia when it is useful. Mix it up a bit and show students that you cared enough to prepare something that was interesting.

Koreli shares his thinking about two teachers and how their use of visuals changed his perceptions of each class. "In my history class, the teacher reads from a slide with like 800 words. Well, not really, but it seems like it. The words are small and we try to copy things down when she's talking. It's crazy. You can't even really listen to the video because you're trying to write. But in my science class, the teacher uses a lot more slides. Like there is one idea on each one and there is a pic that helps us understand what she's saying. I feel like I'm really learning science, and I didn't even like science before. But I'm getting it because the information is clear and there are lots of examples. It's like she took the time to really plan it out for us and then put together information to help us understand it. In history, it's just like a rush of info and we aren't even sure what is important. I check out a lot, really, because I get bored and frustrated."

YOUR PASSION DID NOT CHANGE BECAUSE YOU ARE TEACHING FROM A DISTANCE. MAKE SURE THAT YOUR STUDENTS KNOW THAT.

CREDIBILITY

IMMEDIACY

This final construct of teacher credibility focuses on accessibility and relatability as perceived by students. The concept of immediacy was introduced by social psychologist Albert Mehrabian (1971) who noted that "people are drawn toward persons and things they like, evaluate highly, and prefer; and they avoid or move away from things they dislike, evaluate negatively, or do not prefer" (p. 1). Teachers who move around the room and are easy to interact with increase students' perception of immediacy. That's hard to do in a virtual space. But have you considered visiting their breakout rooms? Have you considered using student names during your live sessions and making sure every student hears their name every day? Teachers need to be accessible and yet there needs to be a sense of urgency that signals to students that their learning is important to you.

1. Get to know something personal about each student, as students know when you don't know their names or anything about them.

2. Teach with urgency but not to the point that it causes undo stress for them. That said, students want to know that their learning matters and that you are not wasting their time.

3. Start the class on time and use every minute wisely. This means that there are tasks students can complete while you engage in routine tasks

such as taking attendance and that you have a series of sponge activities ready when lessons run short. Students notice when time is wasted. And when there is "free time," they believe that their learning is not an urgent consideration of their teachers.

Consider the following examples of general things you can do to ensure that your students feel close to you irrespective of the format of the class:

- Gesture when talking
- Look at students and smile while talking
- Call students by name
- Use *we* and *us* to refer to the class
- Invite students to provide feedback
- Use vocal variety (pauses, inflections, stress, emphasis) when talking to the class

Ashlee Montferret discusses ways to maintain immediacy with students.

First-grade teacher Marco Espinoza uses a puppet in his sessions with students. He finds that this improves his immediacy because his students see him interacting with it. The puppet and Mr. Espinoza have conversations and then invite students to share their thinking. For example, the lesson focused on weather. They had talked about the changes in weather each day and now were focused on the concept of seasons. The puppet kept asking Mr. Espinoza questions about seasons such as "Why does it stay cold so many days in row?" and "How many seasons do we have?" As they talked, students observed. Actually, they were glued to their computer screens. When Mr. Espinoza turned to the class, he said, "Using your hand raising button, who knows the name of the season when summer finishes but it's not winter?" All of the virtual hands went up. Mr. Espinoza invited a student to share. He then invited another student to agree or disagree. And then a third student was invited to say how they knew this. The puppet seemed very excited with the information and asked follow-up questions of the students. This simple tool helped Mr. Espinoza maintain his immediacy with his students.

Carla Balzer is a special education teacher who supports students' learning in their regular classes. In addition, she meets with small groups of students for additional support each day. As she says, "I keep my groups to five so that I can maintain a sense of closeness with them. I usually do some preteaching so that they have background information before they are in class. I also work on vocabulary with them, and we laugh a lot. It keeps us connected. I keep my camera on so that students can see me. And I make sure that I'm looking at them, even when their cameras are off. It's hard, but I think it's really important for them to feel close to me."

CONCLUSION

When a teacher is *not* perceived as credible, students tune out. They fail to log in, they fail to complete tasks, they fail to engage with peers; they fail. And quite frankly, we can't afford for students to do so. We need students to engage, to trust their teachers, and to choose to participate in their learning. The four aspects of teacher credibility—trust, competence, dynamism, and immediacy—can help do just that. As a final task for this module, now that you have a sense of the value of teacher credibility, complete the following self-assessment.

FACTOR	USING THE "TRAFFIC LIGHT" SCALE, EVALUATE YOUR CURRENT LEVEL OF IMPLEMENTATION (GREEN IS GOOD OR REGULARLY; RED IS THE OPPOSITE).	USING THE SCALE BELOW, DETERMINE HOW IMPORTANT THIS FACTOR IS FOR YOU.
Trust		not at all somewhat very extremely
Competence		not at all somewhat very extremely
Dynamism		not at all somewhat very extremely
Immediacy		not at all somewhat very extremely

SUCCESS CRITERIA

- I can develop routines and procedures that ensure that trust is maintained in distance learning.

- I can demonstrate my competence using familiar routines and acknowledge new learning especially related to technology.

- I can bring passion to synchronous and asynchronous learning for my students.

- I can find ways to maintain immediacy with students in distance learning.

- I can support others in developing and maintaining their credibility.

MODULE 5

TEACHER CLARITY AT A DISTANCE

LEARNING INTENTIONS

- I am learning how to increase clarity in distance learning.

- I am learning about learning intentions and success criteria.

Armen Kassabian reads aloud.

Access more videos from Armen at https://tinyurl.com/ hiphopreadalouds. Using a creative pedagogy called Hip Hopnication, this channel includes read-alouds in English, Spanish, and French. Students follow and enjoy the rhythms of hip hop beats while learning new vocabulary and reflecting on the lessons in books through deep questions.

Do your students know what they are supposed to be learning? Or do they see the class as a list of things to do? There is a big difference between these two. When students know what they are expected to learn, they are more likely to learn it. At some point in every lesson, students should know what they are supposed to learn. Before we go much further into this topic, it's important to note the first part of the last sentence. We did not say at the outset of the lessons they should know what they are learning. At some point, they should. There are a number of valid reasons for withholding the purpose, or learning intention, until later. For example, the students in April Hanson's first-grade class were learning about bats. They watched a number of videos and their teacher read aloud several short informational texts. In their live session, Ms. Hanson guided them through a discussion about what they knew about bats and created a graphic organizer. Then, she let them know the purpose of the lesson, which was to write a paragraph about something related to bats that they knew a lot about. The topics included echolocation, their life cycle, different types of bats, their dietary habits, and the different areas in which they lived. The learning intentions did not focus on bats, but rather on writing an informational paragraph about them. Ms. Hanson wanted to build her students' background knowledge before focusing on the expected learning.

There is more to teacher clarity than learning intentions. Fendick (1990) describes four practices that combine to create clarity:

1. **Clarity of organization**: Lesson tasks, assignments, and activities include links to the objectives and outcomes of learning (what we call learning intentions and success criteria).

2. **Clarity of explanation**: Information is relevant, accurate, and comprehensible to students.

3. **Clarity of examples and guided practice**: The lesson includes information that is illustrative and illuminating as students gradually move to independence, making progress with less support from the teacher.

4. **Clarity of assessment of student learning**: The teacher is regularly seeking out and acting upon the feedback they receive from students, especially through their verbal and written responses.

Teacher clarity has a respectable effect size of 0.75. In other words, it's a potential accelerator of students' learning. As we noted with other topics in this book, there are not studies of teacher clarity in distance learning. Instead, we are taking what we know from the classroom and applying it to other environments. Having said that, it's hard to imagine that simply completing a bunch of random tasks will cause learning. If school is reduced to a checklist of things to do, students may complete those tasks without developing a deep understanding of their own learning and the purpose or relevance of that learning.

This module focuses on some of the aspects of teacher clarity described by Fendick. Future modules will focus on other aspects, such as examples and guided practice, assessment, and lesson tasks. In this module, our attention

DRAWING ON MY EXPERTISE

Consider the following questions about your past experiences with teacher clarity.

1. How have I established learning expectations for students?

_____

_____

_____

_____

2. How do I ensure students know what success looks like?

_____

_____

_____

_____

3. How do I align tasks with learning expectations?

_____

_____

_____

_____

4. How do I design assessments of learning expectations?

_____

_____

_____

_____

centers on helping students understand **what they are supposed to learn, why that is important, and how they will know if they learned it**. We have organized this into three questions that contribute to teacher clarity (Fisher, Frey, & Hattie, 2016):

- What am I learning today?
- Why am I learning it?
- How will I know that I learned it?

WHAT AM I LEARNING TODAY?

WHY AM I LEARNING IT?

HOW WILL I KNOW THAT I LEARNED IT?

START WITH THE STANDARDS

Standards represent the official curriculum that schools must provide for students. They guide the instructional decision-making for teachers who work to implement the curriculum. Often, teachers use instructional materials that are aligned with the standards (well, they are supposed to anyway). These materials include textbooks, supplemental materials, and online resources. In some cases, the authors of the instructional materials have analyzed the standards and created learning expectations. Sometimes, they're good and other times they're not so good. And sometimes teachers want to reorganize the materials to create a pathway for learning for their students. To our thinking, teachers have to know the standards for their grade or subject area if they are going to make informed decisions about learning expectations and assessments.

There are a number of ways to analyze standards. A simple way is to take a look at the nouns (or noun phrases) and verbs (or verb phrases) in the standards. This provides clarity about the concepts (nouns) and skills (verbs) that students must master. This analysis can also help teachers understand the type of thinking required or the depth of knowledge needed to be successful. For example, some standards focus one idea, while others on several ideas. And still others focus on how ideas relate to one another or how ideas can be extended.

Let's look at a few examples. We'll focus on one standard at time, understanding that learning units often address multiple standards simultaneously.

Hunter Rogers teaches fourth grade. His team was focused on a language arts standard, which read

Interpret information presented visually, orally, or quantitatively (e.g., in charts, graphs, diagrams, timelines, animations, or interactive elements on web pages) and explain how the information contributes to an understanding of the text in which it appears.

Olivia Amador talks about the importance of teacher clarity in distance learning.

They noted that the concepts students need to learn included

- Information presented visually
- Information presented orally
- Information presented quantitatively
- Charts, graphics, diagrams, timelines, animations, interactive web pages
- Text

And the skills students need to learn included

- Interpret
- Explain
- Contribute to an understanding

A sixth-grade team was focused on the following mathematics standard:

Solve unit rate problems including those involving unit pricing and constant speed.

The concepts included

- Unit rate problems
- Unit pricing
- Constant speed

There was only one skill:

- Solve

A world history standard reads

Explain how the ideology of the French Revolution led France to develop from constitutional monarchy to democratic despotism to the Napoleonic empire.

The concepts include

- Ideology
- French Revolution
- Constitutional monarchy
- Democratic despotism
- Napoleonic empire

AT SOME POINT IN EVERY LESSON, STUDENTS SHOULD KNOW WHAT THEY ARE SUPPOSED TO LEARN.

Kim Elliot and Kasey Woollard talk about looking deeply at the standards to identify what students need to know.

Again, there is only one skill:

- Explain

Are you noticing a trend? There are often many concepts in a standard and only a few skills (and sometimes only one). But the skills are illusive. What does it mean, for example, to *explain* in the context of that history standard? Can you accomplish that skill orally or does it need to be written? What makes for a good explanation? These are the questions that plague teachers and are worthy of much discussion. If the standards are assessed on a summative examination, that can provide some clues about the ways in which policy makers view the skills. But that is not always the case, and lack of understanding about the ways in which skills are taught and assessed can lead to further equity gaps.

NOTE TO SELF

Let's practice. Identify a standard or combination of standards that you will teach. Analyze the standard(s) for the required concepts and skills.

Standard(s)

Concepts (nouns)

Skills (verbs)

 Available for download at **resources.corwin.com/distancelearningplaybook**

CREATE A FLOW OF LESSONS: UNIT PLANNING

When the standards to be taught and mastered have been analyzed, it's time to create a flow of lessons. Which skills or concepts come first? What comes later? In some places, this is called a *learning progression*. There is not one right way to flow lessons, but there are probably wrong ways. Some ideas build on other ideas. Some skills are prerequisites to others. But sometimes the order doesn't really matter and it's more of a personal preference.

Cody O'Connell talks about his thinking relative to the planning template.

Cody O'Connell uses a planning template to create the flow of lessons for his "green" engineering class (see Figure 5.1). A blank version of the planning template can be found in the appendix. It can also be downloaded from this book's companion website for ease of use. Notice that the template is organized for a unit, not a day. We will get to daily learning intentions later. For distance learning, units average two to four weeks. It seems that longer units wear on students and their engagement decreases. Also notice that the planning template includes activities and assessment opportunities as well as instructional materials. Before putting content online, teachers or teams of teachers can pace out the flow of learning to ensure that students have opportunities to master the standards. Further, this template includes a place to address the vocabulary demands of the learning. Teaching vocabulary well is important as words serve as labels for concepts. Understanding a text is significantly influenced by vocabulary knowledge. Writing well is also influenced by vocabulary knowledge. That's probably why the effect size of vocabulary at 0.63 is so strong.

In addition, the template provides an opportunity to describe supports for students with disabilities. Teachers can plan additional supports for other students as well, but our experience with distance learning suggests that teachers must pay special attention to the learning needs of students with disabilities. When teachers plan for these needs in advance, rather than reacting to them later, students are likely to learn more. It's a key principal of Universal Design for Learning (CAST, 2018).

Figure 5.1 Planning Template for "Green" Engineering Class

Standards	Topic (Learning Progressions)	Week	In-Class Activities	Formative Assessment Extend—Review—Assess—Reteach	Texts and Resources

HS-PS2-2 Motion and Stability: Forces and Interactions
 	
Use mathematical representations to support the claim that the total momentum of a system of objects is conserved when there is no net force on the system.
 	
HS-PS3-2 Energy
	Investigation & Model: Balloon Jet System	1	1. Iterative Design Introduction: Tennis Ball Carrier Challenge
			2. Balloon Jet: Engineering Investigation & Model #1
			3. Modeling Introduction & Peer Feedback
			4. Forces & Free Body Diagrams
			5. Improve Balloon Jet Model #2
				1. Flip Grid - Iterative Design Process
				2. Balloon Jet System Model #1 - Assess prior knowledge
				3. Small Group Modeling Feedback & Improvement
				4. Flip Grid - Description of object in motion, forces acting on it, and net force (Free Body Diagram)
				5. Model #2
				  a. Peer and teacher feedback (sticky note critique) on model with forces and free body diagram concepts
					1. Tennis Ball Carrier Device Challenge
					2. Balloon Jet/Rocket
					3. Scientific Modeling: Article
					4. Forces & Free Body Diagrams Stations:
					  a. Free Body Diagrams
					  b. Types of Forces
					  c. Constructing Free Body Diagrams
					  d. Drawing Free Body Diagrams
					5. Balloon Jet Free Body Diagram (image)

HS-PS2-1 Motion and Stability: Forces and Interactions
 	
Analyze data to support the claim that Newton's second law of motion describes the mathematical relationship among the net force on a macroscopic object, its mass, and its acceleration.
 	
HS-PS3-2 Energy
	Newton's Laws & Balloon Boats/Cars System	2	6. Newton's Laws Foldable & Online Investigation
			7. Newton's Laws Applied-Practice With the Laws
			8. Application to Balloon Jet & Comic Strip Model #3
			9. Balloon Boat/Balloon Car Engineering Investigation & Testing
			10. Newton's Laws & Forces in Balloon Boats & Cars Model #4
				6. Newton's Laws Foldable
				  a. Collaborative student and teacher lead group instruction
				7. Newton's Laws Stations
				8. Model #3
				9. Flip Grid - Relationship between Force, Mass, and Acceleration
				10. Model #4
					6. Newton's Laws (articles)
					  a. Live Science
					  b. NASA - Newton's 3 Laws
					  c. Physics for Kids
					7. Newton's Laws Stations:
					  a. Applications (video)
					  b. Practice Problems: 1, 2
					  c. Simulation
					  d. Khan Academy
					8. Comic Strip (template & instructions)
					9. Balloon Boat/Balloon Car & Testing
					10. Discussion Questions

HS-PS3-2 Energy Develop and use models to illustrate that energy at the macroscopic scale can be	Thermodynamics & Steam Engines	3	11. Energy Introduction: Toy Lab & Energy Concept Map 12. Energy Foldable	11. Individual & Group Concept Maps a. With & Without Word Bank 12. Energy Foldable	11. Toy Lab 12. Energy (online resource)

Standards	Topic (Learning Progressions)	Week	In-Class Activities	Formative Assessment Extend—Review—Assess—Reteach	Texts and Resources

accounted for as a combination of energy associated with the motions of particles (objects) and energy associated with the relative positions of particles (objects).
 	
HS-PS3-3 Energy
 	
Design, build, and refine a device that works within given constraints to convert one form of energy into another form of energy.
			13. Laws of Thermodynamics Foldable & Online Investigation
			
			14. Application to Balloon Jet & Comic Strip Model #3
			
			15. Steam Engine Investigation & Model #4
				13. Flip Grid
				
				14. Model #3 (improved)
				
				15. Model #5
					13. Laws of Thermodynamics:
					  a. Khan Academy
					  b. Live Science
					  c. Science Clarified
					14. Discussion Questions
					15. Steam Engine:
					  a. Glass Engine (video)
					  b. Soda Can Steam Engine Boat (instructional video)
					  c. Pop Pop Boat Boiler Engine Example

Week 4: Summative Assessment Competency

Steam Boat: Model & System Explanation

- Steam Boat Comic Strip Model
  - General Modeling Practices
  - Forces & Free Body Diagrams
  - Newton's Laws
  - Laws of Thermodynamics
- Steam Boat Model Explanation
  - 3 Paragraph Explanation connecting concepts to Comic Strip
    - Forces
    - Newton's Laws
    - Laws of Thermodynamics
  - Flip Grid Explanation

(Continued)

CLARITY

Figure 5.1 (Continued)

Content and Academic Vocabulary

- Iterative Design
  - Iterations
- Free Body Diagrams
  - Force
- Newton's Laws:
  - 1st Law
    - Inertia
  - 2nd Law
    - Force, Mass, Acceleration
  - 3rd Law
    - Action & Reaction
    - Laws of Thermodynamics
  - 1st Law
    - Conservation of Energy
  - 2nd Law
    - Entropy
  - 3rd Law
    - "Absolute 0" (Particle Motion)

Accommodations and Modifications for Students With Disabilities

- Cloze style foldables and notes
- Example Scientific Models & Models with blank labels
- Read alouds
- Flip Grid Scripts

NOTE TO SELF

Let's practice. Based on the standard(s) you analyzed, what might be a reasonable order to teach the concepts and skills?

Concepts (nouns)	Skills (verbs)

Flow of Concepts and Skills

1.

2.

3.

4.

5.

6.

7.

8.

CREATE LEARNING INTENTIONS

WE CARE THAT STUDENTS KNOW WHAT THEY ARE SUPPOSED TO BE LEARNING. THIS IS ESPECIALLY IMPORTANT IN DISTANCE LEARNING.

As part of each lesson, students should know what they are expected to learn. These are the learning intentions, which others call *objectives*, *learning targets*, or *learning goals*. There are differences for each of these terms, but we are not interested in the semantics. Rather, we care that students know what they are supposed to be learning. This is especially important in distance learning as students tell us that they get lost in the tasks and are sometimes not sure what they are supposed to be learning. As Ricardo, a tenth-grade student noted, "At school, the teachers always let us know what we're learning. And not just one time. Like many times, they remind us. And we talk about what we learned and what we still need to learn. When I'm online, there aren't as many reminders. And I try to get the work done but sometimes I don't know what I was supposed to be learning and then I don't do so well on the assessment."

As an example of learning intentions, Australian physics teacher Matt Gavin identified three major areas of learning based on his analysis of the standard:

Energy is required to separate positive and negative charge carriers; charge separation produces an electrical potential difference that can be used to drive current in circuits.

Mr. Gavin decided that the flow of learning would be

- Current, potential difference, and energy flow (4 hours)

- Resistance (4 hours)

- Circuit Analysis and Design (6 hours)

For the first segment, he identified several learning intentions. We will not repeat them all here, but here are a few of them:

- I am learning that an electric charge can be positive or negative.

- I am learning about the law of conservation of electric charge.

- I am learning to define *electric current*, *electrical potential difference* in a circuit, and *power*.

- I am learning to solve problems involving electric current, electric charge, and time.

- I am learning to solve problems involving electrical potential difference.

Of course, appropriate tasks will need to be aligned with each of these learning intentions. But that is for later, in Modules 6 and 7.

In distance learning, teachers share learning intentions with students in a variety of ways. For example,

- In a second-grade class, the learning intentions were posted on the opening page in the learning management system.

- In a fourth-grade class, the learning intentions were posted in the chat box during a live session and reposted several times as tasks changed.

- In an algebra class, the learning intentions were introduced at the outset of the video presentation and reviewed several times during the video.

Matt Gavin talks about the development of learning intentions and success criteria.

Crissy Knopp uses a distance learning log with her fifth graders. Based on the planning template, she and her team members identify learning intentions and success criteria (see Figure 5.2). A blank version of this is located in the appendix and is available for download. Students save a copy of the document to their drives and track their progress across the week. For example, as part of a larger unit addressing the standard "Write opinion pieces on topics or texts, supporting a point of view with reasons and information," students were focused on identifying information that supported an opinion. The learning intention was

- I am learning how to use information that supports an opinion.

The form includes success criteria, which we will explore in the next section. In addition, the form includes a space for students to record the tasks that they have completed relative to the learning intention. Ms. Knopp uses "must-dos" and "may-dos" and students know that they can copy the tasks into their doc as they complete them. This allows Ms. Knopp to monitor her students' progress and address needs that she identifies with small groups of students in synchronous learning sessions. She also provides her students with demonstrations via video that they can use on their own as well as examples of previously completed work.

There are a number of ways to create different types of learning intentions. For example, some are related to content and others are process related. Sometimes, the learning is individual and other times it is collective (more information can be found in *The Teacher Clarity Playbook*; Fisher, Frey, Amador, & Assof, 2019). For our purposes here, we'll focus on the individual learning of content, recognizing that teachers will expand on this as their comfort with distance learning increases. At the very minimum, students should know what they are expected to learn for each task they are asked to do. In addition, students should know what success looks like, which brings us to success criteria.

CLARITY

Figure 5.2   Distance Learning Log

Student name:	Content: ELA	Grade: 5

Week of October 14

This Week's Learning Intention(s)	Tasks/Assessments I Completed
I am learning how to use information that supports an opinion.	

Success Criteria

Use the space below to rate your learning before and after each lesson.

Criteria	Before	After
I can find factual information in a text.		
I can sort the information and identify useful information for an opinion.		
I can review the information to make sure that the opinion is valid.		
I can analyze an opinion to determine if the facts support it.		

IDENTIFY SUCCESS CRITERIA

Melissa Noble shares her learning intentions and success criteria with students.

The point of providing students success criteria is to ensure that they know what it means to have learned something. The effect size of success criteria is 0.54, making it another strong accelerator of student learning. There are many ways to ensure that students know what success looks like. In Ms. Knopp's class, "I can" statements are used. In distance learning, we find these to be one of the useful ways teachers can ensure that students know what learning looks like and can monitor their own progress. Of course, Ms. Knopp does not simply list the success criteria on the form for students to download. She also talks about the success criteria in her opening video.

NOTE TO SELF

Let's practice. Based on the standard(s) you analyzed, what might be some learning intentions?

Concepts (nouns)	Skills (verbs)

Learning Intentions

1. _____

2. _____

3. _____

4. _____

5. _____

6. _____

7. _____

8. _____

 Available for download at **resources.corwin.com/distancelearningplaybook**

CLARITY

Mr. Gavin, the physics teacher profiled earlier, also uses "I can" statements. The success criteria for the learning intentions presented earlier include the following:

ITEMS ON A CHECKLIST NEED TO BE UNDERSTOOD BY STUDENTS.

Learning Intention	Success Criteria
I am learning that an electric charge can be positive or negative.	• I can recognize positive and negative charges. • I can summarize the difference between positive and negative charges.
I am learning about the law of conservation of electric charge.	• I can explain what the law of conservation of electric charge means for an isolated system. • I can define the law of conservation of electric charge in my own words. • I can write the law of conservation of electric charge.
I am learning to define *electric current, electrical potential difference* in a circuit, and *power*.	• I can describe (in my own words) *electric current, electrical potential difference* in a circuit, and *power*, and how they relate to each other. • I can recognize that electric current, electrical potential difference in a circuit, and power are related to circuits.
I am learning to solve problems involving electric current, electric charge, and time.	• I can determine values for current, electric charge, and time in complex situations. • I can recall that electric current is equal to the amount of charge movement per time. • I can calculate current in a simple circuit when charge is known and time is known.
I am learning to solve problems involving electrical potential difference.	• I can determine values for electric potential difference in complex situations. • I can recall the formula for calculating electric potential difference. • I can calculate the electrical potential difference between two points.

In addition to "I can" statements, teachers can use checklists, rubrics, exemplars, and modeling to ensure that students know what success looks like. In some content areas, these are more effective than "I can" statements. For example, in writing, the use of a checklist can help prevent formulaic pieces. Of course, items on a checklist need to be understood by students. Consider the following fifth-grade writer's checklist:

- Topic is introduced effectively.

- Related ideas are grouped together to give some organization.

- Topic is developed with multiple facts, definitions, or details.

- Linking words and phrases connect ideas within a category of information.

- There is a strong concluding statement or section.

- Sentences have clear and complete structure, with appropriate range and variety. Knowledge of writing language and conventions are shown.

- Any errors in usage do not interfere with meaning.

Marnitta George shares success criteria using a checklist and rubric.

Of course, some of these are subjective. But "good" writing is hard to describe and it takes practice and feedback to develop strong writing skills.

The students in Haley Miller's class used this checklist on a regular basis to improve their writing. Before they submitted a piece for peer review, they analyzed their own writing to identify areas that still needed work (and feedback) and areas that they believed were strong. Ms. Miller also provided exemplars for students to analyze as mentor texts, some of which were strong examples and others that were not so effective. As Ms. Miller notes, "It takes time, patience, and a lot of feedback to really improve writing. My students use the checklist as a self-assessment and then they use it to provide peer feedback. I also have individual writing conferences with students using video conferencing to talk through what I see. I ask them a lot of questions about the checklist so that they come to understand what success looks like. Sometimes, I share my screen and show them another piece of writing. I talk through what I see in this other piece so that they may be able to use it to improve their writing."

Note that Ms. Miller used both a checklist and exemplars to ensure that her students understood what success looked like. She also modeled her thinking for some students as she read their papers. For example, while reading Nayeli's paper, Ms. Miller said,

> Nayeli, the introduction of your paper reminds me of Andrew Clements, and we really like his writing. For me, as your reader, you really captured my attention right from the start. I'm wondering why you didn't think your introduction was effective, but we can come back to that in a minute. What I am noticing is that you present a fact and it was really interesting. But I noticed that it was just one fact. The checklist talks about multiple facts, definitions, or details. But I only see one. I'm thinking that you know more about this topic, especially from the power of your introduction. What are you thinking about now?

Their conversation continued but note in this short snippet the ways in which Ms. Miller modeled her thinking so that her student would develop a better understanding of what success looked like. Again, there is not one right way to ensure that students know what success looks like. We encourage you to try out different options and see which of them work for you. You will know you're successful when students know what learning looks like.

NOTE TO SELF

Let's practice. Based on the standard(s) you analyzed and the learning intentions you developed, what might be some success criteria?

Concepts (nouns)

_____

_____

_____

_____

_____

_____

_____

_____

Skills (verbs)

_____

_____

_____

_____

_____

_____

_____

_____

Success Criteria

1. _____

2. _____

3. _____

4. _____

5. _____

6. _____

7. _____

8. _____

 Available for download at **resources.corwin.com/distancelearningplaybook**

A VIEW FROM THE EARLY YEARS

By Claudia Readwright

Thinking about teacher clarity brings a few anecdotes to mind. Some years I haul out the overhead projector and adjust the focus to show them what I see without my glasses . . . it is like looking through waxed paper. "If I want to see clearly, do you think I should leave my glasses in the case or wear them?" Other years, I show two beakers of water, one with clean water and one filled with pond water. "If we want to see through the beakers, which one would be better, clear or cloudy?"

One way to demonstrate clarity and relevance to young learners is the Brain-File Cabinet Analogy. In physical school, I have them gather around a two-drawer file cabinet and tell them our brain is like a file cabinet. Every time we learn something, we either start a new file or put the information into a file we already have in the drawer. To continue the lesson, I draw their attention to the three art prints I have hung behind the cabinet. I chose van Gogh's "Starry Night," Ringgold's "The Sunflower Quilting Bee at Arles," and Marc Chagall's "I and the Village." (One of the standards this lesson addresses is the CA Preschool Foundation AF1.0, or DRDP Measure COG 2 or Kindergarten State Standard KMD.A.1.) You can imagine how to adapt this in virtual class. I provide each child 3 x 5-inch mini prints of the three artworks as their voting paddles. Instead, you might have the prints numbered and have the children vote by holding up the correct number of fingers or they can call out "Chagall!" I explain we are going to sort and classify items that relate to our art prints. I hold up a package of sunflower seeds, or a photo of a constellation or a violin. The votes fly up to their computer screens. I ask why they chose that print. We can discuss in smaller groups in a breakout room, answer alphabetically in whole group, or pull name sticks.

I knew the Brain-File Cabinet Analogy was clear when I told my kindergarten children we were going to make a sarcophagus. I looked into a sea of confused faces. When I asked, "Does anyone know what a sarcophagus might be?" Taqqert pulled an imaginary file drawer out of his forehead, and began to rifle through his files, saying "sarcophagus, sarcophagus, sarcophagus . . . I've got nothing." Everyone laughed. I asked, "Do you have an Egypt file?" He pulled the drawer out again and said "Wait! Does it have something to do with a mummy?"

One of the ways that I ensure children understand the criteria for success is to have them take responsibility for creating the rubrics. Yes, first-grade students can do this. Students kept digital portfolios, so we had past projects to show younger students some possible ways to demonstrate understanding. When stating our learning intention, children would begin calling out suggestions. "Can we make a vocabulary quilt like we did for Harriet Tubman?" "What about a tableau?" Eventually, children would employ the "*Maybe* . . . Thinking Routine. Maybe we could . . . !" "Yes, Mzilikazi! Maybe we could—and add a musical part to it!" They learned to scale their projects to other classes or groups. Children know what criteria illuminates success. In order to get a 4 on the quilt project, you needed to know your square, and the squares of your three group members. Their criteria was much more stringent than I would have

(Continued)

(Continued)

assigned. Each child makes a can for their "I can" statements. Once the project is finished, they speak through their can like a megaphone. "I can describe my quilt square and define my word as well as all three of my team member's words and squares." When it comes to learning intentions, they can tell you that they are learning to identify what makes a work clearly that of Marc Chagall's. If you ask them how they know, they might tell you, "I look for common objects like a goat, or a violin, or floating people."

I announce our Study (which is a unit) and ask the children to volley back and forth all the things they know about the topic. We teach children to volley by partnering up and giving a beanbag. When we volley, we say one fact and toss the beanbag to a friend. They say a fact and toss it back. In distance learning, we can demonstrate "volley" by wearing two puppets and tossing the beanbag between the puppets. In our insect study, we learned about insects in a general sense and then narrowed the focus to individual insects. After the volley, we create our KW(L) chart. We list the things we know and then the Wondering column becomes the springboard for our daily questions. This practice ensures the learning is relevant because the questions come directly from the student's wonderings. "I wonder where butterflies go at night or when it rains." In distance learning, we can relay that question to the family and then have our shared discussion and writing the next meeting.

FIND THE RELEVANCE

As we have noted before, boredom has a significantly negative impact on learning, with an effect size of -0.47. To counter that, teachers need to make learning relevant for students. Students who have high levels of self-regulation tend of find relevance in a lot of the learning they're introduced to. Students who have low levels of self-regulation need help finding relevance. What is relevant to one person may not be relevant to another. Priniski, Hecht, and Harackiewicz (2018) conceptualize relevance across a continuum from least to most relevant. We have defined these as follows:

- **Personal association** is through a connection to an object or memory, such as enjoying a reading about travel because the student recalls riding in an airplane when she was younger. Similarly, association occurs when a student makes a connection with something outside the classroom and thus wants to learn more.

- **Personal usefulness** is derived from a student's belief that a task or text will help them reach a personal goal. For example, a child reads articles about soccer because he wants to improve his passing skills. Or a student perseveres through a mathematics course because she believes that the knowledge will help her gain admission to a specific college, thus allowing her to study engineering.

- **Personal identification** is the most motivating type of relevancy, and stems from a deep understanding that the task or text aligns with one's identity. When students get to learn about themselves, their problem-solving, and their ability to impact others, relevance is increased. For example, a student who wants to build shelters for stray cats is highly motivated to learn geometry. A student who sees herself as a poet seeks feedback and lessons about voice, ideas, and organization.

Jessica Bradford teaches second grade. She knows that her students are generally engaged in their learning. They like learning and love stories. When she introduces a new story to her students, she asks them why we focus on the characters. The range of responses on a given day included

- Because we want to write stories, too.

- Because when we see how characters feel we understand why they do things.

- Because characters help us think about our behavior.

- Because characters have emotions and so do we.

As you can just imagine, the students sat with rapt attention to their screens as their teacher started to read. The lesson was relevant because students understood that they could reach their goals in participating in this lesson.

Similarly, the students in Jerrod Barlow's middle school science class find relevance in their lessons when their teachers talk with them about why they are learning certain things. He tries to make connections with students' personal identification. For example, in their unit on human body systems, Mr. Barlow regularly made connections to sports and fitness goals, healthy living, and future careers, all things that his students had told him were important. For example, he said, "Our next system focuses on the brain and we all know how important that is. But did you know that you can change your brain? Like literally. You can change what is inside your head. It's about the connections inside our brains. Really, you can change it. Like tonight. Want to know how?" As you can imagine, they all put their virtual thumbs up, ready to learn.

Oscar Corrigan talks about making distance learning relevant for students.

CONCLUSION

Teacher clarity is an important consideration in developing distance learning opportunities for students. We can't forget that students in *any* school environment need to know what they are learning and how they will know if they are successful. Further, addressing the relevance of the lesson can engage students. We'll spend more time on engagement in the next module.

Teacher clarity is more than learning intentions and success criteria, as we will explore further in this book. But they are important components for ensuring that students learn. The learning intentions and success criteria are derived from the standards and teacher-made decisions about the effective flow of information for students' learning. As a final task for this module, now that you have a sense of the value of teacher credibility, complete the following self-assessment.

FACTOR	USING THE "TRAFFIC LIGHT" SCALE, EVALUATE YOUR CURRENT LEVEL OF IMPLEMENTATION (GREEN IS GOOD OR REGULARLY; RED IS THE OPPOSITE).	USING THE SCALE BELOW, DETERMINE HOW IMPORTANT THIS FACTOR IS FOR YOU.
Analyzing standards		not at all somewhat very extremely
Developing learning units and flowing lessons		not at all somewhat very extremely
Creating learning intentions		not at all somewhat very extremely
Identifying success criteria		not at all somewhat very extremely
Finding relevance		not at all somewhat very extremely

SUCCESS CRITERIA

- I can describe various aspects of teacher clarity.

- I can use the three clarity questions to plan distance learning experiences.

- I can analyze standards to identify concepts and skills.

- I can develop learning intentions that ensure students know what they are supposed to learn.

- I can develop success criteria that provide students ideas about what learning looks like.

- I can discuss the relevance of the learning expectations with students.

MODULE 6

ENGAGING TASKS

**LEARNING
INTENTIONS**

- I am learning
  about
  historical and
  contemporary
  models of
  engagement.

- I am learning
  about
  functions
  and tools
  for distance
  learning.

MANY OF
US HAVE
WITNESSED
THIS
FIRSTHAND
AS STUDENTS
SWITCH OFF
MICROPHONES
AND CAMERAS
IN ORDER TO
TURN THEIR
ATTENTION TO
SOMETHING
ELSE.

Engagement is at the core of learning. Disengaged students learn less and are often negatively labeled as "unmotivated" or "a behavior problem." Without question, a disengaged learner may well be a bored one. With an effect size of −0.47, boredom is a powerful decelerator to student learning. Many of us have witnessed this firsthand in virtual learning sessions as students switch off microphones and cameras in order to turn their attention to something else. However, we wonder to what extent the achievement gap discussed in policy papers and school staff meetings is really an engagement gap.

Gauging student engagement is more than just cataloging who is turning in their assignments or leaning forward in their seats with eyes on the teacher. Engagement has historically been understood across three dimensions: behavioral, cognitive, and emotional engagement (Fredricks, Blumenfeld, & Paris, 2004). It turns out that these are too inter-related and thus are not very predictive of student success. Of course, if a student is sleeping, they can't engage. Following this review of a historical model of engagement, we'll turn to a more compelling model that presents engagement along a continuum, which we find more compelling from a learning perspective.

Behavioral engagement is the dimension most commonly referenced when describing a student's engagement. These are observable academic actions that teachers instantly recognize. Two items are a student's level of participation in class and submission of assignments. But behavioral engagement alone is an insufficient gauge. We perceive students who know how to "do school" in online and face-to-face classrooms as engaged. But Windschitl (2019) defines *doing school* as "rote and shallow learning performances, which students and teachers give to each other to signify that they are accomplishing normative classroom tasks" (p. 8).

Cognitive engagement provides further nuance to what it means to be engaged with learning. Now we're talking about the psychological effort students exert to master content. Students who seek challenge and self-regulate are said to be cognitively engaged. Observable actions include

- Planning

- Monitoring their own progress

- Setting goals

- Solving problems

Emotional engagement is the *affective* dimension of learning. Interest and relationships contribute to a student's ability to learn. Learners who have a sense of belonging and have an affinity toward classmates are more likely to

- Engage in discussions

- Pose questions

- Seek help when needed

- Exhibit curiosity about a subject

We invite you to activate your prior knowledge about how you address each dimension instructionally and in your curricular design.

DRAWING ON MY EXPERTISE

What instructional techniques and curricular design approaches do you use to engage students in each dimension?

	INSTRUCTIONAL TECHNIQUES	CURRICULAR DESIGN
Behavioral engagement		
Cognitive engagement		
Emotional engagement		

 Available for download at **resources.corwin.com/distancelearningplaybook**

Figure 6.1 A Continuum of Engagement

ACTIVE ← _____ PASSIVE _____ → ACTIVE

Disrupting	Avoiding	Withdrawing	Participating	Investing	Driving
Distracting others Disrupting the learning	Looking for ways to avoid work Off-task behavior	Being distracted Physically separating from group	Doing work Paying attention Responding to questions	Asking questions Valuing the learning	Setting goals Seeking feedback Self-assessment

DISENGAGEMENT	ENGAGEMENT

Marisol Thayre talks about student engagement along a continuum.

Amy Berry (2020) interviewed teachers about the conception of engagement, and most often they saw engagement more in terms of "doing." The focus seemed to be whether or not the students engaged in doing the task. Of course, we can have observable cues of students engaging in doing tasks. Berry called this _participating_, but many teachers wanted more. This led to her model with three forms of engagement and three of disengagement. According to Berry, students can move between these forms. Naturally, we all want to help students move from participating or "doing" to investing and driving their own learning (see Figure 6.1).

THINK FUNCTIONS OF ENGAGEMENT, NOT JUST TOOLS

It can be intimidating to keep track of all the technology tools available for use by teachers and students in a distance learning environment. Educators around the world experienced this anxiety to varying degrees in the rapid move to distance and remote learning. As we scrambled to find ways to re-create our classrooms in a virtual environment, the focus in many cases was on the tools themselves. How to install and operate took precedence over whether these tools were actually useful to teachers and students. So, let's take a deep breath and recall what it is that students need to be able to accomplish in their learning (Frey, Fisher, & Gonzalez, 2013, p. 1):

- _Find information_ efficiently and be able to evaluate whether the information is useful, credible, accurate, and corroborated by other sources.

- _Use information_ accurately and ethically.

- *Create information* such that its creation deepens one's understanding.

- *Share information* responsibly with audiences for a variety of purposes.

As noted previously, it isn't the medium that matters. Information is manipulated verbally, with paper and pencil, and through interpretive dance, for that matter. A collaboratively constructed document by a group of students could happen with a chart paper and a handful of markers, or it could occur online using web-based software. These functions transcend the spaces in which they are enacted and serve as a foundation for thinking about the ways to engage learners. You won't find a long list of web-based tools in this playbook, as innovative ones seem to blossom weekly. By shifting the attention from the tools (which are cool and seemingly infinite) to the *functions*, we can hone what we need to accomplish in order to build students' capacity in face-to-face and distance learning. The functions of learning lead right back to the engagement in learning (see Figure 6.2 for examples).

Christian Capetillo talks about functions and tools.

Figure 6.2 Functions and Tools

	Engagement Opportunities	Sample Tools
Finding Information	- Can locate information sources - Can organize and analyze information sources for accuracy and utility to the task - Locating information is driven by curiosity	- Kahoot - MindMeister Add-On - Quizlet - Padlet - Twitter - Google
Using Information	- Can cite sources of information - Makes judgments about how best to use information - Asks questions the information provokes	- Evernote - Flipgrid - Grammarly - PlayPosit
Creating Information	- Can write and discuss information according to grade-level expectations - Transforms information in order to explore ideas new to the learner - Takes academic risks to innovate	- Google Docs - ThingLink - Tik Tok - TurnItIn
Sharing Information	- Accurately matches purpose to audience - Uses metacognitive thinking to identify the best strategies for the stated purpose - Is resourceful and resilient	- Animoto - Storybird - Tik Tok - Remind - WeVideo - YouTube

SET THE CONDITIONS FOR ENGAGEMENT AND LEARNING

LET'S TAKE A DEEP BREATH AND RECALL WHAT IT IS THAT STUDENTS NEED TO BE ABLE TO ACCOMPLISH IN THEIR LEARNING.

Astute educators know that all that is taught is not necessarily learned, regardless of the setting. The quest, then, is to determine what ingredients are vital for learning to occur. We ask ourselves, what is the right combination of experiences that ensure learning? What conditions must be present? Teachers whose mission it is to cultivate engaged learners teach the kinds of strategies learners need and create opportunities for students to use them. They hold a metaphorical mirror up to students to promote reflection, self-questioning, problem-solving, and decision-making. These teachers mediate the thinking of their students as often as they possibly can, so that their students can gain more insight into how and when they learn and associate their actions to results. And they possess a clear vision of the kind of learner they are building because they know the characteristics of an engaged learner: behaviorally, cognitively, and emotionally.

SELECT THE TOOLS THAT MEET THESE FUNCTIONS AND CONDITIONS

Selecting a limited suite of tools can be challenging, as there are so many to choose from. We will confess that we have seen too many endless lists of tools and resources to scroll through. However, they don't also offer guidance in how to curate a manageable number of tools that will address the learning functions you need to optimize engagement levels. Here are some considerations as you make decisions on which tools make the most sense for your context. Many learning management systems (LMS) come with built-in tools, which doesn't mean you need to use them all. In addition, school districts have their own guidelines about how external tools can be utilized, and under what conditions. Having said that, here are some questions for consideration, whether examining LMS built-in tools or those that are on external sites (see Figure 6.3). You can find additional copies of this template on this book's companion website.

Some of the questions you should consider include the following:

- What learning function does this tool fulfill?

- Is it developmentally appropriate for my students to use with minimal adult assistance?

- Does this tool have accessibility features that are aligned to digital compliance requirements (e.g., provides closed captioning, supports screen-reader software)? What are they?

What conditions are necessary in order to perform these functions in face-to-face classrooms? In distance learning?

	FACE-TO-FACE CLASSROOMS	**DISTANCE LEARNING CLASSROOMS**
Finding information		
Using information		
Creating information		
Sharing information		

ENGAGEMENT

Figure 6.3 Evaluation of Distance Learning Tools

Name of Tool _____

Question	Answer
What learning function does this tool fulfill?	
Is the tool/site developmentally appropriate for my students to use with minimal adult assistance?	
Does this tool have accessibility features that are aligned to digital compliance requirements (e.g., provides closed captioning, supports screen-reader software)? What are they?	
Key Features Checklist ☐ A way to prerecord lessons and directions ☐ A written or video-based discussion forum for students ☐ A means for students to submit work ☐ A way to provide feedback to students about their work ☐ A way for students to provide feedback to one another ☐ Assessment tools that allow for formative and summative evaluation ☐ A way to host individual meetings with students, families, and other professionals ☐ A way to share and communicate with other teachers	

online resources ➘ Available for download at **resources.corwin.com/distancelearningplaybook**

In addition, you need productivity tools that allow you to perform major teaching functions. Again, many LMS platforms offer features for grading online and such. In addition, Figure 6.3 includes a key features checklist. You don't necessarily need all of the functions listed on the checklist, but they are aspects you may want to consider.

Our point is that you will want to avoid overwhelming your students and yourself with too many tools. Select them judiciously; better yet, select them as grade-level teams, departments, and schools so there is consistency for students and collegial support for you. Introduce and teach the tools you have selected such that you aren't clustering them too closely together. After all, you wouldn't teach students everything they need to know about your classroom on the very first day. Think judiciously and phase in the tools you'll be using so you aren't overwhelming your students' capacity or yours.

This shows up in the virtual classroom that you create. Laura Hancock created a virtual classroom that reflected her passion about her students' learning.

A virtual Bitmoji classroom is an interactive space for students to click hyperlinks to resources, such as websites, documents, lessons, assignments. As Dr. Hancock noted, "I would like to know about this, but I thought, is it difficult and will it take a lot of time? Or is it just a cutesy thing that doesn't hold value? I decided that my virtual classroom will be a shell in which I can easily change the content, and that's what makes it a fun and informative way to deliver digital learning instruction."

Dr. Hancock continues, "I wanted to provide a space to hold resources needed for learners' capstone presentation format called PechaKucha, which uses a 20 × 20 format to tell a story or research visually, with 20 slides and 20 seconds of one's own commentary (PechaKucha 20×20, n.d.)." She created this in Google Slides. It has an introduction with screencasting that orients students to new content, which is the PechaKucha presentation format, and how to use it (Chen, Vargas, Thompson, & Carter, 2014). She used Loom for screencasts to make the content easily accessible and provide a visually interesting presentation. Loom is free, cloud based, and easy to edit. All resources are located in the virtual bookcase through hyperlinks. The hyperlink to PechaKucha CREATE is the tool/video that demonstrates how to produce this type of presentation, and in the bookcase are PDF links for the assessment rubric and tips for this type of presentation format. Additionally, there are resources with hyperlinks to Splash and Pixabay for free quality images to support their visual research story and another one for Canva, which allows students to create infographics or design posters to further support their message. Dr. Hancock says, "I also included a PechaKucha example that informs the students of why and how to create great slides. My virtual classroom was converted from Google slides into a pdf and then uploaded to Canvas. Ultimately, my virtual classroom delivers a flexible, accessible, and motivating online environment."

Now it is your turn to itemize what you have and what you need for your virtual classroom. We will use the analogy of being an effective grocery shopper. You make a weekly list of the meals you'll prepare, then do a scan of your pantry and refrigerator to see how much you have and what you will need. Every shopper has a budget, so get what you need and resist the urge to fill your cart up too full.

Laura Hancock demonstrates her virtual classroom.

NOTE TO SELF

Scan your virtual classroom tools: What will students need? What will you need?

	YES	NOT YET	DON'T NEED
Video recording for lessons and directions			
Discussion forum for students			
Student work submission			
Feedback tool			
Formative and summative evaluation			
Individual meeting platform			
Sharing professional learning with colleagues			

 Available for download at **resources.corwin.com/distancelearningplaybook**

DESIGN TASKS WITH ENGAGEMENT IN MIND

The tasks students complete, whether synchronously or asynchronously, should foster learning. Tasks that are busy work, keeping hands busy but minds turned off, are not going to deliver the kind of learning that keeps students engaged, moving from doing to driving as Berry (2020) would put it. Too often students are asked to do an inordinate amount of rote learning with little rationale for why the learning is occurring. Practice is important, of course, and students need to memorize information in order to perform more challenging tasks. Young children need to know the alphabet, recognize words, and manipulate numbers. Unfortunately, too many online tasks seem to be focused on recall and recognition tasks at the expense of other kinds of learning.

Learning remotely doesn't need to be reduced to completing endless amounts of worksheets. The tasks students complete in the company of one another or independently have the potential of fostering engagement through thoughtful design. The South Australia Department for Education and Child Development (2019) supports teachers through professional learning geared toward making tasks more engaging in order to deepen learning. Their recommendations transcend settings:

Hilda Martinez demonstrates some early literacy learning tools.

- **Encourage students to think in more than one way by transforming from closed to open tasks.** Examine the task by looking for ways students can enter from more than one entry point, or by considering more than one perspective. For example, pose problems to students that can be solved in multiple ways.

- **Move from information to understanding by requiring students to connect and relate.** Design some tasks so that students need to compare and contrast two phenomenon, identify rules and patterns, and figure out when seemingly dissimilar ideas are actually related.

- **Ask students what they think first, rather than telling them what they will need.** Create tasks that allow students to try out their ideas first to see what works and what doesn't. For instance, ask students what might work best to resolve a problem, such as a dilemma a character in a story is facing, before reading what the character did.

- **Position students to plan a way forward by moving from procedure to problem-solving.** Foster a group's reliance on one another by providing them insufficient information at first, giving them only some of the steps, or including some irrelevant information.

Tasks designed with these principles in mind can increase engagement, whether performed independently or in collaboration with others. Primary educator Claudia Readwright designs tasks for her youngest students to do with their families. They can then talk about their experiences when they are together. Her at-home learning menu (see Figure 6.4) keeps the focus on the major functions while giving children engaging tasks that allow them opportunities to solve problems, ask questions, and draw on their creativity.

Figure 6.4 At-Home Learning Menu

Eat breakfast, make your bed, get dressed, brush your teeth.
Tell your grown-up how you are feeling today.

Happy	Sad	Excited	Afraid	Tired

iStock.com/Prostock-Studio	iStock.com/beyhanyazar	iStock.com/max-kegfire	iStock.com/shapecharge	iStock.com/Sergey Nazarov

AT-HOME LEARNING MENU 2
Garden

Monday: Sunflowers and van Gogh's Birthday!

Shared Discussion	Letters and Sounds	Math
It's Vincent van Gogh's birthday. We will celebrate by having a Sunflower Day. Tell what you know about sunflowers. Are they tall or small? What color? How did they get their name? The word sunflower has two syllables. Say "sun" in one hand. Say "flower" into the other. Say "sunflower" as you clap your hands.	Think of words that rhyme with *sun*. Did you think of *bun, fun, pun* (a little joke with words that sound the same), *run*, or *sun*? (*Done, none, hon* are rhymes but aren't spelled like our family of words.) Write these words in your journal and add a little drawing so you can use them when you write another day.	Guessing Jar: Invite children to explore a small jar filled with sunflower seeds. They have a chance to examine the jar and estimate how many seeds are in the jar. "Look at the sunflower seeds in a jar. Do you think you can guess how many are in there?" Write down the guess. Open the jar and count. How close to the number was your child's guess?

Fine Motor	Art or Sensory	Gross Motor
Pinch sunflower seeds and drop them into one cup of an empty egg carton. Put 10 in each cup. Have someone help you count to 100 by 10s (or 120 if you can!).	Create a sunflower. You can draw with yellow, orange, green, brown, and black crayons or colored pencils. If you have paints, create a sunflower with a long stem.	Garden, Yoga-Flower Pose: Lift your bent legs, balancing on your sitting bones. Weave your arms under your legs, palms up. Pretend to be a flower in bloom.

Tuesday: What Do We Know About Gardens? What Do We Want to Learn?

Shared Discussion	Letters and Sounds	Math
What is a garden? A garden is a place where plants such as flowers, fruit, and vegetables grow. Read a book about gardens. Talk with your family about their experience with gardens. Do you have a garden?	Say "garden"—clap two syllables while you say "garden." Who in our family has a two-syllable (clap) name? What else starts with "g"? Draw in your journal and label. Did you think of grass? Grasshopper? Green? Gloves?	Roll a Garden: Roll a die. Use red and draw that many lines for garden rows on a 6 × 6-inch paper. Roll again; use orange crayon to draw that many rows. Roll die; draw that many yellow rows. Roll the die for green rows. Which has more rows? Fewer?

Fine Motor	Art or Sensory	STEM
Use playdough to make daisies. Use a flattened ball for the center. Flatten more balls for the outside. Roll a snake for the stem. Use smaller balls for leaves. Count petals and leaves.	Paint/draw a garden. Try using colors in rainbow order. Red flowers, then orange, yellow, (green) blue, and purple. Add green leaves. Poke holes in an old water bottle cap.	Make a watering can out of an old jug or water bottle. Punch holes in the screw top. Put water in the bottle and use to water plants.

Wednesday: What Grows Out of the Ground?

Shared Discussion	Letters and Sounds	Math
Explain that plants such as flowers, fruits, and vegetables grow out of the ground. List your ideas. Sing "The Gardener Builds the Fence."	After finding pictures of fruits and vegetables in grocery ads and magazines, choose at least four to draw and color. Label with their beginning sound or sound out the whole word.	Make a counting book using the fruit and vegetable pictures you drew. Put the book in order: 1 apple, 2 bananas, 3 ears of corn, 4 . . . etc. Print the number in the corner.

Fine Motor	Art or Sensory	Gross Motor
Cut out pictures of things that grow from the ground. Look in grocery ads and magazines. Sort the pictures into categories of fruits, vegetables, or herbs. Draw your favorite in your daily journal.	Make seed packets. Label the packet with the name and what the fruit or vegetables will look as grown produce after harvest. **STEM** Grow a carrot top in a dish. Keep track of growth in journal.	Go on a walk. Take your list from Shared Discussion. See how many of the things on you list you find. Do you find plants growing in soil or dirt? Pots? Planters? Walk. Hop. Jump.

Thursday: Helpers and Pests in the Garden

Shared Discussion	Letters and Sounds	Math
What do the worm and the snail bring to the garden? Is one a pest and one a helper? Have someone write down your questions and let's find out!	Think of rhymes for *snail*. Did you think of *bail, fail, hail, jail, mail, pail, sail, tail*? Write these words in your journal and add a little drawing so you can use them when you write another day.	Play a game of HighLow. Use playing cards with number cards. (Leave out face cards.) Ask your grown-up to pass out cards evenly between two players. Set half the deck in front of each of you, and turn over the top cards. High card wins both cards.

Music	Art or Sensory	STEM
Sing a Song of Flowers (Tune: "Sing a Song of Sixpence"): Sing a song of flowers, Flowers all around. Flowers that are growing, Growing in the ground. Flowers of each color Make a pretty view. Red and orange and yellow Blue and purple, too!	Draw spirals with a black crayon and use watercolors to paint a snail shell. If you do not have watercolors, you can put a dried-out marker in a little cup and the ink will make watercolor wash.	Set up a warm habitat. Get a clean jar. Put holes in lid. Put shredded newspaper on the bottom, then soil into the jar. Find worms. They are easy to find after it rains. Gently put them into the jar. Put some orange peels and strawberry slices under the soil.

Friday: Gardeners and Tools

Shared Discussion	Letters and Sound	Math
What does a gardener do? What kind of tools does a gardener use? Is one trowel better than another? What kind of garden hose is best?	Draw your favorite garden tool. Think of the beginning sound. Try to label your tool. Tell why your chose that tool. Try out the tool and draw what you looked like being a gardener.	Set out playing cards in order in a line on the floor. Count out objects to match that number. 1 is one penny, 2 is two pennies, 3 is three pennies.

Fine Motor	Art or Sensory	STEM
Strengthen your pincher fingers and weed the flowerbed. Ask your grown-up if it is a weed before pulling. Strong pinchers make better writers.	Draw around leaves with a crayon. Press hard. Draw the veins on the leaves. Use watercolor to paint over crayon. The crayon will resist the paint.	Gather snails from the yard. Put them in an empty container with holes in the lid. Put some decaying leaves and fresh leaves in for them to eat. Which do they prefer?

Source: Claudia Readwright. Used with permission.

By Claudia Readwright

A VIEW FROM THE EARLY YEARS

Our Early Learning Department consciously decided to offer two different formats to our young learners and their families. We knew that many families had more than one child who would be accessing our district's learning guides through our "Exercising Your Brain" link (https://www .fresnounified.org/learningguides#brain). Therefore, we knew we needed to provide families with flexible options.

Both formats mirrored the district's K–6 learning guides. The first provided a suggested schedule and included activities for each discipline similar to a typical school day. The other format was designed as a menu. The menu offered tasks where every member of the family could participate in the learning. This could ease the pressure on some parents who suddenly found themselves in the role as instructor of a multi-age classroom!

After a twenty-five-year career successfully teaching in a project-based classroom, I knew the nature of open tasks would be the answer. An art piece by one of the masters serves as a springboard for an entire week. The day would begin with a shared discussion including an opportunity for writing. Each box on the menu could be chosen a la carte or in tandem with any of the other choices. I pictured caregivers reading the six offerings and asking the child which two they might like to do before lunch. The menu was made available the Friday before the following week. That way, if the family wanted to participate in an experience that included a resource they did not have, they had the weekend to gather the materials. In Figure 6.4, you can see that sunflower seeds (not something typically found in every home) would be used for a couple of the garden activities. During the week, there is an opportunity to connect and relate by studying two sunflower prints to compare and contrast the artistic compositions. STEAM projects were offered so the children could test out their ideas and would involve varied age groups if desired. Once their ideas were tested, opportunities to build upon the outcomes could be carried forward. These asynchronous experiences at home give us the opportunity to engage with students and their families in meaningful ways through distance learning.

NOTE TO SELF

Use the task design principles to match to four different online tasks you currently use.

An open task

An understanding task

An asking task

A problem-solving task

DESIGN A CONSIDERATE SCHEDULE TO PROMOTE ENGAGEMENT

Teachers and students have experienced the "Zoom exhaustion" that comes from too many hours trying to sit still and remain engaged in front of a screen. Some schools initially tried to replicate schooling in real time using schedules that were designed for face-to-face instruction. They quickly found out that five or six hours of daily instruction, complete with the same bell schedules, recess breaks, and lunch schedules, was not workable. One reason is because homes don't run on a school schedule, and the burden placed on families made it nearly impossible for them to manage. Another is that our own homes don't work that way, either.

The time we are in front of students in live sessions should be prioritized for connection, discussion, and interaction. That means that some learning should occur asynchronously, rather than in real time. When planning lessons, think about learning experiences students need to prepare them for the interactive discussions you host in a virtual setting. These might be readings, short videos for students to preview, or written tasks that leverage prior knowledge.

Consistency and predictability of schedule are student and family friendly. Design weekly schedules that provide students with expectations about tasks to be accomplished before and after live sessions. Be sure to include the learning intentions, success criteria, and any assessments so that students have a clear sense of purpose and can ask questions in advance. High school mathematics teacher Heidi Allen provides her students with digital sticky notes to sort as teams. In preparation for an assessment, teams sorted them according to their level of confidence, which allowed her to use targeted reteaching as needed (see Figure 6.5).

A scheduling template for the learning in grade-level or schoolwide use can help tremendously in providing students with consistent and predictable ways to engage with the content, with you, and with their peers. A template such as the one in Figure 6.6 is particularly useful for families with several children attending a school, and at the secondary level for students who are meeting with several subject matter teachers. It's not that students complete all of the tasks at the bottom of the page, but rather that they know when they are responsible for which things.

One mistake we made early on was in not giving attention to conflicting schedules. We quickly realized that while teachers were doing their best to schedule sessions, the result was that students and families couldn't possibly juggle meetings that changed each day. And what is a student supposed to do when the English teacher and a special education support person were unknowingly asking for the same time? We shifted to specific days of the week so that live sessions for each subject are evenly spaced. Just as a bell schedule

Staci Benak shares her thinking about consistency.

Jacob Hampson talks about the use of a distance learning planner.

Hayley Sampson shares her use of the distance learning planner.

Figure 6.5 Ms. Allen at Work in Her Distance Learning Mathematics Class

Source: HSHMC.

Photo: Kim Elliot.

is useful to all of us in a brick-and-mortar school, so is a scheduling template in a distance learning environment.

A schedule that is inconsistent and unpredictable is going to provoke behavioral disengagement. Think back to the indicators we outlined at the beginning of this module:

- Participating in school functions
- Attending and participating in class activities and discussions
- Following school rules
- Studying
- Completing assignments

There are students who have difficulty doing this in face-to-face classrooms. But how much organizational structure do we provide for those students? It is even more important when students are at a distance and the interactions are in virtual spaces.

Jean Lawton talks about meeting with students with disabilities individually and in small groups to support their success in their classes.

Figure 6.6 Distance Learning Weekly Planner

Content: _____ Grade: _____

Week of: (DATE) _____

This week's Learning Targets/Intentions	Tasks/Assessments	Success Criteria
I am learning . . .		I can . . .

Monday	Tuesday	Wednesday	Thursday	Friday
Attend:	Attend:	Attend:	Attend:	Attend:
Read:	Read:	Read:	Read:	Read:
Watch:	Watch:	Watch:	Watch:	Watch:
Discuss:	Discuss:	Discuss:	Discuss:	Discuss:
Turn in:	Turn in:	Turn in:	Turn in:	Turn in:

online resources 🔗 Available for download at **resources.corwin.com/distancelearningplaybook**

NOTE TO SELF

What scheduling issues are you taking into consideration at your school?

When will you hold synchronous sessions? How frequently? For how long?	
How will asynchronous learning bracket live sessions (before and after)?	
What do families need in order to be supportive (but not to burden them with doing school themselves?	
How will students access technology help?	
How will you collect family questions and concerns?	
How will you coordinate your efforts with other educators?	

 Available for download at **resources.corwin.com/distancelearningplaybook**

ENGAGEMENT

CONCLUSION

The next normal in schooling requires that we build the capacity of our students and ourselves to shift fluidly between mediums in order to keep learning moving forward. This can be partially accomplished in face-to-face classrooms using blended learning approaches. However, in order to foster our collective capacity in all settings, we need to proactively consider these functions and the conditions that support them across platforms and foreground them with intention. As a final task for this module, self-assess to rank factors related to engagement. This will allow you to target your professional learning efforts.

FACTOR	USING THE "TRAFFIC LIGHT" SCALE, EVALUATE YOUR CURRENT LEVEL OF IMPLEMENTATION (GREEN IS GOOD OR REGULARLY; RED IS THE OPPOSITE).	USING THE SCALE BELOW, DETERMINE HOW IMPORTANT THIS FACTOR IS FOR YOU.
Gauging dimensions of engagement		not at all — somewhat — very — extremely
Thinking functions, not just tools		not at all — somewhat — very — extremely
Setting the conditions for engagement and learning		not at all — somewhat — very — extremely
Selecting the tools that meet these functions and conditions		not at all — somewhat — very — extremely
Designing tasks with engagement in mind		not at all — somewhat — very — extremely
Designing a considerate schedule to promote engagement		not at all — somewhat — very — extremely
Greeting students		not at all — somewhat — very — extremely
Learning students' names and how to pronounce them		not at all — somewhat — very — extremely
Learning about their interests		not at all — somewhat — very — extremely

SUCCESS CRITERIA

- I can design tasks that move students from "doing" to "driving."

- I can describe the functions for which I will select learning tools.

- I can evaluate tools for their usefulness.

- I can use the task design principles in distance learning situations.

- I can develop and implement a considerate schedule.

ENGAGEMENT

MODULE 7

PLANNING INSTRUCTIONAL UNITS FOR DISTANCE LEARNING

We care about student learning and believe that there is no one right way to teach. If students are learning at least one year of content for each year in school, we're happy. We believe too much talk has focused on teaching and not enough on learning. Having said that, educators do need to design meaningful learning experiences that provide students with opportunities to learn. As we have noted before, teachers should not hold an instructional strategy in higher esteem than their students' learning. Thus, this module focuses on a framework for instruction and we provide examples of instructional routines that teachers might find useful. Importantly, these are examples. If they do not work for your students, please change them.

Jesse Lin's seventh-grade students were being introduced to their book clubs. As part of this unit, he wanted students to do the following as part of his learning intentions:

- Expand their skills in inferencing.

- Develop and support a written argument in response to a question connected to their book club.

Mr. Lin created a video in which he talked about each of the books. He read aloud from the first page of the book to demonstrate the writing style and modeled his thinking about the vocabulary of each book. Students then voted on the book that they would like to read. He created groups and students scheduled times to meet with their groups to talk about their readings. The sessions were recorded for Mr. Lin to review, but he regularly joined the groups to guide and facilitate their discussions. Students were asked to respond to daily writing prompts to practice their composing and Mr. Lin provided students feedback on their responses. The final essay focused on the class essential question, "Does age matter?" and students used information from their text and their own experiences to answer the question. The students would load their responses into the class learning management systems which provided the opportunity for two peers to review their papers before Mr. Lin graded them.

The individual choices that Mr. Lin made instructionally worked for him and impacted his students' learning as evidenced by their change in writing performance, measured on a rubric. Mr. Lin monitors progress across the year to see the impact of each unit on students' writing. But the individual strategies are less important. What is more important is the framework that guides his decision-making. Did you notice that Mr. Lin provided a demonstration? His read aloud provided students an opportunity to see their teacher read and hear his thinking. He also ensured that his students had opportunities to collaborate. Further, he facilitated and coached the thinking of his students and provided them with opportunities to practice. And all of this was based on what he wanted students to learn, the learning intentions and success criteria, or purpose for learning. Figure 7.1 contains a visual of the instructional framework that guides the design of lessons.

LEARNING INTENTIONS

- I am learning to design experiences that impact students' understanding.

- I am learning how various strategies align with different aspects of distance learning.

AS WE HAVE NOTED BEFORE, TEACHERS SHOULD NOT HOLD AN INSTRUCTIONAL STRATEGY IN HIGHER ESTEEM THAN THEIR STUDENTS' LEARNING.

DRAWING ON MY EXPERTISE

Consider the following questions about your past experiences with quality instruction.

1. How do I provide students input and information?

_____

_____

_____

_____

2. How do I structure collaborative tasks?

_____

_____

_____

_____

_____

3. How do I guide students' thinking?

_____

_____

_____

_____

_____

4. How do I ensure students practice and apply what they have learned?

_____

_____

_____

_____

_____

Figure 7.1 Instructional Framework

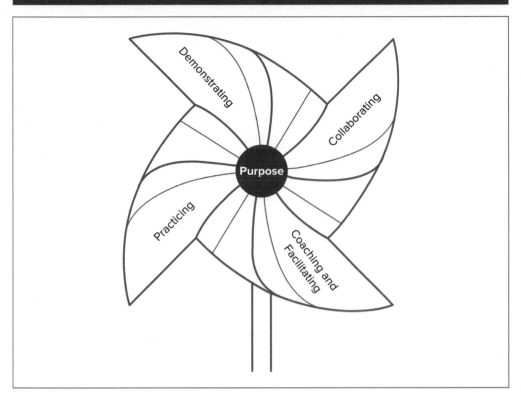

As you may have noticed, the center of the pinwheel is the purpose or intention for learning. As we noted in Module 5, teacher clarity plays a significant role in students' learning. In fact, it drives the instructional decisions that teachers make. The tasks students are assigned must be aligned with the goal for learning. Also, the purpose for learning helps teachers make decisions about how to use instructional minutes. Thus, all of the other parts of the pinwheel metaphorically spin around the pin in the middle, which is the purpose.

In planning for distance learning, unlike a lesson for which there is a set time such as a literacy block or social studies class, teachers must consider the various ways and times that students will access the class. In some cases, there are synchronous and asynchronous learning opportunities spread across a week. In other cases, there are daily expectations for students. As you think about your plan, consider the strategic use of each of the four blades (or aspects) of the pinwheel: demonstrating, collaborating, coaching and facilitating, and practicing. Below, we will delve into each of these aspects more deeply.

WHAT IS MOST IMPORTANT IS THE FRAMEWORK THAT GUIDES YOUR DECISION-MAKING.

DEMONSTRATING

Demonstrations provide students with examples of what they will do or learn. This aspect of learning provides students with a glimpse inside the mind of another person. Often this is the teacher, but it does not have to be. For example, a

PLANNING

student in an art class recorded a time-lapse video of her drawing and narrated the final version, sharing her thinking about what she was doing over time. This demonstration provided other students with an example that they could use as they created their own pieces. The point was not to produce the same drawing as the one shared by the student demonstrating, but rather to climb inside her mind and understand her thinking.

There are a number of ways that teachers can demonstrate for students:

- Direct instruction
- Think-alouds and think-alongs
- Worked examples
- Lectures
- Share sessions

Each of these approaches allows the person demonstrating to share his or her thinking with others. Just showing someone how to do something does not ensure that they can do it later. How many times have you seen someone cut hair, change a tire, or bake a cake, still not sure you can do it yourself? Imagine the difference if someone shared the thinking involved in each step of the process (and then allowed you to practice and receive feedback). That might just make the difference for you to be able to own that learning.

Thinking is invisible. A major aim in classes is to help make this thinking more visible such as by using these four methods. Our cognitive processes become apparent to others primarily when we speak or write. Many of the concepts and skills we teach are abstract. Sharing thinking with students allows them a glimpse into the inner workings of our brains as we process and act upon information. The research world calls this a *think-aloud* but we worry that this term focuses exclusively on the teacher, so we like to use the phrase *think-along* to ensure that students are engaged in the process as their teachers think aloud.

THINK-ALONGS

Our experience has been that off-the-cuff think-alongs tend to be unfocused and can leave students more confused. A planned think-along ensures a higher degree of clarity. Resist the urge to clutter your think-alongs with too many divergent ideas—it shouldn't be a stream of consciousness. We used the following guidelines (Fisher, Frey, & Lapp, 2009) to plan and record robust think-alongs about a passage from George Orwell's *Animal Farm* that we recorded for students to view (and view again, if needed):

- **Name the strategy, skill, or task.** "I'm going to think out loud about how I noticed repetition in this passage."
- **State the purpose of the strategy, skill, or task.** "Good speakers who are giving a speech will often repeat a key idea or two again and again. It makes the message stick."

THE TASKS STUDENTS ARE ASSIGNED MUST BE ALIGNED WITH THE GOAL FOR LEARNING.

Bryan Dale models his thinking while reading.

- **Explain when the strategy or skill is used.** "The first thing that got me noticing that there was going to be some repetition coming was in the first line of the first paragraph: 'And remember, comrades.' Major is telling the other animals that something important is coming next because he is telling them that this is going to be something important to remember."

- **Use analogies to link prior knowledge to new learning.** "It's like when I see a politician giving a speech at a rally. They have a slogan and they repeat it over and over so you remember it long after the speech is over."

- **Demonstrate how the skill, strategy, or task is completed.** "I'm going to show you the repetition I saw in the first paragraph. First, he says, 'Never listen. . . .' Then he says, 'It is all lies.' Then at the end of the paragraph he says again, 'All men are enemies. All animals are comrades.' Three times in one paragraph he repeats the same idea: Don't listen to Man. He can't be trusted. All Men are the enemy.' I noticed this because the repetition was so close together."

- **Alert learners to errors to avoid.** "Speakers can use repetition pretty effectively, but I know I have to be on the lookout for how a repeated message can change. It's like the telephone game when you whisper a message to one person, who then whispers it to another. By the time it gets back to the first person, the message is completely different. I look for repetition, but I also have to keep an eye out for how the message might change when other speakers use it."

- **Assess the use of the skill.** "So, I'm going to make a note in the margin that there is some repetition happening, and I am going to highlight those sentences where I saw it happening. I want to be able to come back to the original message to compare it if others use a similar message. I want to be able to see if it has stayed the same or if it has changed."

JUST SHOWING SOMEONE HOW TO DO SOMETHING DOES NOT ENSURE THAT THEY CAN DO IT LATER.

A planning tool for think-alongs can be found in Figure 7.2. Think-alongs, as with most other forms of demonstrating, are delivered using first-person language. This spoken language mirrors one's own internal dialogue. These "I" statements can feel awkward at first, but they contribute to a think-along's effectiveness by triggering empathetic listening on the part of the student. It is human nature to respond emotionally to such statements. The use of "I" statements invites students into the thinking process in ways that second-person directives do not. Consider the difference between the two:

- **First-person statement:** "When I read this term, I'm confused so I scan back up to the bolded definition in the previous paragraph to remind myself what it means."

- **Second-person statement:** "When you run into an unfamiliar term, remember to scan back up and reread the bolded definition."

The first example gives students insight into the use of a comprehension strategy as it is deployed during the act of reading. The second, while good advice, uncouples the strategy from the decision to use it. Novice learners don't just need to know what the strategy is—they need to know when to apply it.

Figure 7.2 Think-Along Planning Template

Component	Places in the Text and Language to Be Used
Name the strategy, skill, or task.	
State the purpose of the strategy, skill, or task.	
Explain when the strategy or skill is used.	
Use analogies to link prior knowledge to new learning.	
Demonstrate how the skill, strategy, or task is completed.	
Alert learners to errors to avoid.	
Assess the use of the skill.	

online resources   Available for download at **resources.corwin.com/distancelearningplaybook**

DIRECT INSTRUCTION

Direct instruction is another way to demonstrate for students. To be sure, direct instruction has gotten a bad rap in some quarters. In fact, it might be one of the most misunderstood instructional approaches out there. Impressions about direct instruction usually cluster into three categories:

1. It is scripted and didactic.
2. It is inflexible.
3. It devalues teacher judgment.

Hilda Martinez uses direct instruction with her young learners from a distance.

With an effect size of 0.59, direct instruction offers a pedagogical pathway that provides students with the modeling, scaffolding, and practice they require when learning new skills and concepts. Rosenshine (2008) noted that the structure of a direct instruction lesson should follow a pattern that includes the following:

1. Begin a lesson with a short review of previous learning. Going from the known to the new is powerful.
2. Begin a lesson with a short statement of goals.
3. Present new material in small steps, providing practice for students after each step.
4. Give clear and detailed instructions and explanations.
5. Provide a high level of active practice for all students.
6. Ask a large number of questions, check for student understanding, and obtain responses from all students.
7. Guide students during initial practice.
8. Provide explicit instruction and practice for seatwork exercises and monitor students during seatwork.

UNFORTUNATELY, THERE ARE MANY CLASSROOMS IN WHICH TEACHERS DO ALMOST ALL OF THE TALKING. ONE OF THE RISKS WITH DISTANCE LEARNING IS THAT TEACHERS REPLICATE ALL OF THAT TALK ONLINE.

WORKED EXAMPLES

A **worked example** is a math problem that has been fully completed to show each step of a mathematician's arrival at a solution. These have been shown to be useful for students in completing problems more efficiently and accurately and have an effect size of 0.37. It is important, of course, to identify from the beginning whether a worked example is correct or erroneous. Worked examples that are erroneous as well as those that are correct can spark student thinking as they hypothesize why the mathematician made the decisions they did to arrive at a solution. Worked examples are not limited to use in mathematics. Teachers can share their thinking about writing, art, lab reports, and many other worked examples. Essentially, the teacher (or another student) thinks aloud about an example that has already been completed using "I" statements as we noted before. The goal is to share your thinking and develop students' mental models so that they incorporate that type of thinking into their own practices.

NOTE TO SELF

How can I use direct instruction in my distance learning classes?

What concept or skill do my students need?

What is the goal for the lesson?

How can I explain this to students?

How can I ensure that they practice as I observe?

How can I teach them so they can then teach others?

 Available for download at **resources.corwin.com/distancelearningplaybook**

Another advantage of using worked examples is that they help reduce the cognitive load on students. Remember most of us struggle to remember more than four to six things at once, our working memory is limited, and we want students to focus on the most important parts of the lesson and not be distracted by the lesser important parts. As we show worked examples, there can be a "expertise reversal effect" as students start by listening to explicit instruction and dialogue from the teacher and begin to incorporate this thinking and explanations as part of their own skills and conversion to longer-term memory. They can hear the problem-solving and reduce their focus on the redundant parts; and this is also the core of the gradual release of responsibility by the teacher.

LECTURES

Of course, teachers can also record their **lectures** and demonstrate their content knowledge for students. Lectures should not go on and on, especially in a virtual environment and should include opportunities to check for understanding. Chemistry and biology teacher Angie Hackman uses an integrated quiz feature in her video lectures to check students' understanding. When they answer incorrectly, the system requires that they re-watch the section and answer again.

SHARE SESSIONS

Teachers can use **share sessions** in which we visually show students how to do something. For example, see the video of Shayna North engaging her nutrition students remotely in a cooking lesson. Her students had been provided a home delivery of the supplies and cooked alongside her in their own homes.

Heidi Allen demonstrates a worked example for her students.

Angie Hackman uses an integrated quiz feature in her video lectures to check students' understanding.

Shayna North engages her nutrition students remotely in a cooking lesson.

NOTE TO SELF

How can I use worked examples, lectures, or share sessions in my distance learning classes?

PLANNING

COLLABORATING

STUDENTS NEED TO BELIEVE THAT THEIR GROUPS WILL IMPACT THEIR COLLECTIVE AND INDIVIDUAL LEARNING AND SEEK EVIDENCE OF THE IMPACT OF THEIR EFFORTS.

One of the teacher mindframes we value is "I engage as much in dialogue as monologue." Unfortunately, there are many classrooms in which teachers do almost all of the talking. One of the risks with distance learning is that teachers replicate all of that talk online or even increase the amount of talk so that they can fill the space. But the second aspect noted in our pinwheel of instruction is **collaborating**. We believe that students should be provided time to engage in dialogue with their peers. And we believe that these dialogues between and among students are powerful ways to improve learning. In fact, the effect size for classroom discussion is 0.82. These meta-analyses do not include evidence from online discussions, but we think that the same rules generally apply. For example, the task has to be complex enough to warrant more than one person. Further, students need to believe that their groups will impact their collective and individual learning and seek evidence of the impact of their efforts.

An important consideration is when to invite students to dialogue with the teacher and with each other. We recommend that they do so once they have acquired sufficient knowledge and begin to grapple with the relations between ideas. That's the ideal time to ask them to take more ownership or regulate their own learning. This is when the power of listening to others, thinking aloud themselves, and querying, justifying, exploring, and being curious are most successful.

There are a number of routines that have been tested in physical classrooms that teachers are adapting for distance learning. These include book clubs, text rendering, jigsaw, and reciprocal teaching. Of course, there are many other collaborative routines that can be used in distance learning, not to mention a wide range of tools, such as Google docs, sheets, and slides, that allow students to interact with their peers. Such technology is now ever present and it seems many schools have adopted a set of these tools; we do not recommend any particular suite or set of software—our interest is what you do with them as teachers and as learners.

For example, the students in Krista Jenkins's first-grade class had been asked to bring an item from their home that started with the letter *t* to the class meeting. They scattered to find the item and returned to their laptops. Ms. Jenkins placed the students in partners and invited them to share their item and talk about it. This first step was designed for oral language practice. Bringing the students back together as a whole class, Ms. Jenkins asked a student to talk about the item that their classmate shared. She said "timer."

Ms. Jenkins wrote the word on her screen, which was being projected. She sounded out the word as she wrote it, saying, "What a great word. It starts with our letter *t* and it has one of the patterns we are learning. We know the word *time* and we can add the *r* sound." Her lesson continues as students share the item their peer brought to the meeting. Of course, Ms. Jenkins had sent information to families in advance in her weekly newsletter so that the items would be appropriate for their letter work.

What collaborative routines will work given my students, my content, and the tools that I have?

BOOK CLUBS

Fifth-grade teacher Carolina Cervantes uses books linked to a common theme and invites her students to choose which they will read. For example, when studying westward expansion, the options included *Riding Freedom* (Ryan, 1998), *Across the Wide and Lonesome Prairie* (Gregory, 1997), *Caddie Woodlawn* (Brink, 1935), *Prairie Visions: The Life and Times of Solomon Butcher* (Conrad, 1994), and *Sing Down the Moon* (O'Dell, 1970). She chose these books based on differing viewpoints related to gender, region, and position, and made sure to include both informational and fictional accounts. After hearing about each book, students rank the order of preference, with Mrs. Cervantes having a final say in the composition of each group.

In an effort to promote reflective conversations in an online environment, she expanded the Discussion Director's role. Each Friday, Mrs. Cervantes gave the day's Discussion Director a list of questions to introduce to the class. On one Friday, they received these questions:

1. What was our best discussion this week? Why?

2. What was the hardest discussion we had? Why?

3. How will we use what we learned about our best discussion and our hardest discussion to improve next week?

The students reading *Riding Freedom* quickly agreed that the best discussion they had was on Wednesday, when they met to talk about the chapter when Charlotte, the protagonist, is revealed to the other characters as a girl, and not the boy Charlie that she had pretended to be.

"I couldn't wait to talk to you," said Tonio, "because I wanted to hear what you thought about it." After reveling in their memory of a compelling discussion, Lapresha, the Discussion Director, asked the second question. After a long silence, Adriana said, "I guess that would be Monday." She then admitted that she had forgotten to read the chapter over the weekend so she couldn't really participate. Two other students immediately confessed to the same thing, and after looking at one another they giggled in embarrassment. "It wasn't fair that we let each other down," offered Lapresha. "You can't talk about a book you didn't read."

The third question now flowed more quickly, as the students realized that the best thing to do next was to remember to do the reading this weekend. "I can call anyone, if they want me to," volunteered Adriana. "I promise I won't forget!"

Did you notice how the productive collaboration and feedback occurring in this classroom encouraged the students to continually improve as they initiated plans for future work?

TEXT RENDERING

Broc Arnaiz introduces text rendering to students.

Sometimes the goal of the group interaction is to identify key ideas from a text. The **text rendering** protocol is useful in this situation and is easily adapted to distance learning. Essentially, students read the text in advance and then meet to "render" it. Here is the protocol:

1. As they read, students are asked to identify an important *sentence*, *phrase*, and *word* and place them into an online collaborative document. These have to be from different parts of the reading.

2. When they meet in the live session, they each take a turn sharing their sentence.

3. Then they take turns sharing their phrases.

4. Finally, they share their words.

5. Then they discuss what they have noticed about patterns in their selections.

The person who is farthest to the left on the video display is the person who keeps the conversation going.

When students meet in groups without a protocol like this, they may not know how to start and may wander from the text. In this case, the words in the collaborative document foster the conversations they have. And they know that they will be required to summarize their understanding of the text on their own when the discussion is over.

JIGSAW

In essence, **jigsaw** is an approach in which students are members of two different groups: a home group and an expert group. Each time they meet with a group, there are different purposes and tasks. Over the course of the jigsaw, students deepen their understanding of the text and have opportunities to develop and practice their communication and social skills. The effect size of jigsaw is 1.20— super powerful, when done well. There are many ways to implement the jigsaw, but it's key that students talk with others during the process. Indeed, it was not created for online learning (it was invented in the arts), but seems built for distance and remote learning. It's not just divide-and-conquer reading in which the text is divided up and students tell each other what they read. For example, consider the following implementation of an online jigsaw.

THE EFFECT SIZE OF JIGSAW IS 1.20–SUPER POWERFUL, WHEN DONE WELL.

The students in Brad Carmichael's class were reading from their digital copy of the textbook for their sixth-grade social studies text. The chapter focused on hunter-gatherer societies. Here's how it worked:

Step 1: In their expert groups, which they could do themselves off-line, each student had been assigned the same section of the chapter. They read this and were asked to consider several questions:

- What do you not understand or are confused about?
- What makes sense to you?
- What do you want to know more about?

They shared their responses to these two topics with other members of their expert groups in a breakout room. They collaborated to ensure that each member of the group had a working knowledge of the section of the text they had been assigned.

Step 2: Each member of the group had been assigned a letter and when the timer was up, Mr. Carmichael regrouped students so that all of the *G*s were together, all of the *J*s were together, and all of the *L*s were together (he selects random letters so that students don't think that they are in the *A* group). The students were each asked to join their unique chat room and share with the others in their new (home) group their thinking about their assigned section. Their peers, who had not read that section, highlighted and added digital comments to that section. They specifically talked about what made sense and what did not. The purpose was to summarize the big ideas.

Step 3: Students returned to their original expert groups or chat rooms and reported back what they learned in step 2. They talked about how their part of the text fit in with the whole text. They looked for similarities and differences and other relationships between the ideas in the text.

Step 4: In this case, Mr. Carmichael added another step and invited each group to report what they learned to the whole class. Mr. Carmichael also could have then asked them a task that used the knowledge and understanding they had derived from this first round—as at minimum all students had been exposed to the main ideas, engaged and heard content, knew subject matter vocabulary, and had been introduced to the characters in this part of the text.

Reciprocal Teaching. Another collaborative task that works in a distance learning format is reciprocal teaching (Palincsar & Brown, 1984). The effect size for reciprocal teaching is 0.74. In this routine, students are assigned a comprehension strategy: predicting, summarizing, clarifying, or questioning. Each group stops at predetermined times to share their thinking using the strategy that they have been assigned.

Stacy Palgrove uses reciprocal teaching in her online biology class. She shares documents with her students that include stopping points for their discussions. Ms. Palgrove's students are required to video record their conversations and submit them to her on the class learning management system. Ms. Palgrove uses a rubric to provide students feedback about their discussion (see Figure 7.3). As Ms. Palgrove notes,

> My students can schedule their reading and discussion any time during the week that they want. But I do want to see the video recording to provide feedback and to ensure that they are engaged in respectful conversations with each other. Some of my students do this late at night, which is fine with me. I just want to make sure that they are reading

THE EFFECT SIZE FOR RECIPROCAL TEACHING IS 0.74.

so that their background knowledge and vocabulary grows. For some students, I send the document with a voice recording so that they can hear me read it. For other students, I record an introduction so that they have more information. With distance learning, I can provide some additional scaffolds and no one else in the class needs to know.

Importantly, appropriate scaffolding has an effect size of 0.58. As Ms. Palgrove notes, when teachers are able to provide a range of scaffolds, students learn more. Further, cooperative learning has an effect size of 0.40. This aspect of distance learning has the potential to accelerate students' performance when done well.

Figure 7.3 Internet Reciprocal Teaching Dialogue Rubric

RT Strategy	Beginning 1	Developing 2	Accomplished 3	Exemplary 4	Score
Questioning	Generates simple recall questions that can be answered directly from factors or information found within the website's home page.	Generates main idea questions that can be answered based on information gathered by accessing one or more links to the website's content.	Generates questions requiring inference. Facts and information must be synthesized from one or more links to the website's content and combined with prior knowledge.	Generates questions flexibly that vary in type, based on the content read and the direction of the dialogue.	
Clarifying	Identifies clarification as a tool to enhance understanding and initiates clarification dialogue when appropriate.	Identifies appropriate words for clarification with the dialogue's context.	Assists group in clarifying identified words based on context clues.	Uses strategies for word clarification that can be applied generally across reading contexts.	
Summarizing	Summary consists of loosely related titles.	Summary consists of several main ideas but also many details.	Summary synthesizes main ideas, is complete, accurate, and concise.	Summary is accurate, complete, and concise, incorporating content vocabulary contained in the text.	
Predicting	Demonstrates knowledge of predictions as an active reading strategy.	Directs group predictions to set a clear purpose for reading.	Articulates predications that build logically from context.	Provides justification for prediction and initiates confirmation or redirection based on information located in text.	

Source: Teach New Literacies. Retrieved from https://teachnewliteracies.wordpress.com/internet-reciprocal-teaching/

NOTE TO SELF

How can I use jigsaw or reciprocal teaching with my students?

By Claudia Readwright

A VIEW FROM THE EARLY YEARS

Prompting dialogue and conversation is a primary goal when designing experiences for young distance learners. We want them to think closely and use their growing language skills. When we study *The Ballet Class* painted by Degas, I tell the children we are going to *See, Think and Wonder* about what's going on in the picture. I follow up with, "What do you see that makes you say that?" I might say, "I am wondering about the woman in the blue dress reading the newspaper. Who is she? What is she doing at the ballet class?" I ask them to use the "Maybe . . ." "Maybe," a child offers, "Maybe she is the dance teacher's wife and she's waiting for a ride home." What do you see that makes you say that? They offer different responses: She looks like she has waited a long time. She looks the same age as the man. We have a grand conversation about waiting, rides home, husbands, wives, for example. At the end of the session, we ask, "What did we learn after studying the painting by Degas?"

Then it's time to write. Using direct instruction, I model the first criteria (writing matches the picture) with a split screen showing two different drawings, labeled 1 and 2. One is of a picnic at the river and the other of ballet dancers on a stage. The sentence at the top says *The dancers wore their tutus.* We ask, "Which drawing matches the sentence?" They vote using one or two fingers. "What do you see that makes you say that?" Discussion follows. We set our goal. "So, today you are going to draw and write something that matches your drawing." I record the instruction and make a slide show using those photos. I've already notified families in the weekly news that they should photograph this writing and send it tomorrow.

I share their writing with the class during our next meet-up. I might use the TAG strategy (see Figure 7.4) with the projected slide and have a child in the audience raise their hand and offer to **T**ell something they noticed about the featured author's work. Another child might **A**sk something about the work. They might **G**ive a suggestion or compliment. Once that criteria is established, we would model the other criteria the same way. Other criteria on our poster include spaces between words, starting sentences with a capital letter, ending with appropriate punctuation, and details to enrich our writing. The featured writer sets their goal and we move on to the next writer's work.

Collaborative routines extend thinking and language. We conduct book clubs using the Loom app to read stories with interesting characters. Post the recordings in advance of your online meet-up and ask, "Which character were you most like?" The children can draw in their journal or reply using the Flipgrid video format. We tally and group the children based on their replies for the arranged meet-up. We might have all those who chose the cricket to meet in breakout 1, and the butterfly in breakout 2. Discussion follows as we gather back in the main room. You need a second adult to facilitate the conversation in the other room. Be sure the adults switch part way through so everyone gets equal access.

COACHING AND FACILITATING FOCUSES ON GUIDING STUDENTS' THINKING WHILE AVOIDING THE TEMPTATION TO TELL THEM WHAT TO THINK.

Figure 7.4 TAG Strategy

T		Tell the writer something you like.
A		Ask the writer a question.
G		Give the writer a suggestion.

Source: Claudia Readwright. Used with permission.

iStock.com/fonikum

PLANNING

COACHING AND FACILITATING

Joseph Assof talks about the challenges of questioning in online learning.

THERE ARE TIMES IN WHICH TEACHERS MEET WITH GROUPS OF STUDENTS FOR COACHING. IN THIS CASE, TEACHERS MEET WITH A SMALL GROUP OF STUDENTS, BASED ON THEIR IDENTIFIED LEARNING NEEDS.

Speaking of scaffolding, this aspect of distance learning is one of the primary ways that teachers can support students. Often, this is done with small groups or individuals. Essentially, this aspect of the learning focuses on guiding students' thinking while avoiding the temptation to tell them what to think. This requires that teachers ask the right question to get the student to do the work and teach the students how to ask powerful questions. Questioning has an effect size of 0.48.

It is also noted, however, that teachers dominate the class in terms of questions, and questions are the second most dominant teaching method after teacher talk (Cotton, 2001). The estimates of questions per day vary between 100 and 350 (Brualdi, 1998; Clinton & Dawson, 2018; Levin & Long, 1981; Mohr, 1998) and the responses from the teacher questions to the students is typically some form of recall of facts, judgment, or correction, primarily reinforcing in nature, affirming, restating, and consolidating student responses. In over 80 percent of the teacher questions, they already know the answer (Shomoossi, 2004); most of the questions are closed with low cognitive demands on students (see Asay & Orgill, 2010; Erdogan & Campbell, 2008; Nystrand, Wu, Gamoran, Zeiser, & Long, 2001); and the most common form of interaction is still the IRE cycle: *initiate* a question, get a *response*, and teacher *evaluate* the response. "Authentic questions, like uptake, also contribute to coherence. By asking authentic questions, teachers elicit students' ideas, opinions, and feelings, and in so doing, they make students' prior knowledge and values available as a context for processing new information. (thus they) . . . contribute to the coherence of instruction by enlarging the network of available meanings in the class" (Nystrand, Gamoran, & Carbonaro, 1998, p. 19).

One of the downsides of questioning whole classes is the low participation by many students in the question answering. Randolph (2007) found that response cards were powerful in increasing participation (by 50%) and were preferred by students (82%) to hand raising. Response cards are cards, signs, or items that are simultaneously held up by all students in the class to display their responses to questions or problems. Students using response cards, on average, performed higher on quizzes ($d = 1.08$) and higher on tests ($d = 0.38$) in the response card condition than in the hand-raising condition.

We are impressed with Marty Nystrand and colleagues' (1998) notion of the "uptake" question where teachers (or students) validate particular student ideas by incorporating their responses into subsequent questions; and "authentic" questions whereby questions are asked to obtain valued information, not simply to see what students know and don't know. These authentic questions are questions without "prespecified" answers, and like uptake questions, also aim to contribute to coherence.

When questions fail to ensure success, teachers can rely on prompts and cues. In general, prompts are statements made by the teacher to focus students on the cognitive and metacognitive processes needed to complete a learning task. Metacognitive strategies have an effect size of 0.55. When teachers provide prompts, their students apprentice into cognitive and metacognitive thinking.

For example, fourth-grade teacher Marcia Longfellow said to a group of students during their video meeting, "I'm thinking of the video we watched that showed what life was like when the Missions were being built." In this case, she provided a background knowledge prompt. Later, she said, "I'm thinking about what we don't yet fully understand and what we can do to figure things out," which is a reflective prompt focused on metacognition. Four common prompts with examples are provided in Figure 7.5.

Cues, on the other hand, are designed to shift a student's attention. Sometimes, students need this level of support to work through something that is confusing. For example, Missy Stein was working with a group of students and they seemed to miss the exponent in the problem. She used the highlight function on the virtual whiteboard to shift her students' attention to that part of the problem and it worked. As one student said, "OMG, I totally missed that. I thought it was a mixed fraction and it's an exponent." Again, the teacher does not simply tell the student what to think, but rather shifts the learner's attention to something that is likely to help. Figure 7.6 includes a list of common cues and examples.

Figure 7.5   Types of Prompts

Type of Prompt	Definition	Example
Background knowledge	Reference to content that the student already knows, has been taught, or has experienced but has temporarily forgotten or is not applying correctly	• When trying to solve a right-triangle problem, the teacher says, "What do you recall about the degrees inside a triangle?" • As part of a science passage about the water cycle, the teacher says, "What do you remember about states of matter?" • When reading about a trip to the zoo, the teacher says, "Remember when we had a field trip to the zoo last month? Do you recall how we felt when it started to rain?"
Process or procedure	Reference to established or generally agreed-upon representation, rules, or guidelines that the student is not following due to error or misconception	• When a student incorrectly orders fractions thinking the greater the denominator, the greater the fraction, the teacher might say, "Draw a picture of each fraction. What do you notice about the size of the fraction and the number in the denominator?" • When a student was unsure about how to start solving a problem, the teacher said, "Think about which of the problem solving strategies we have used that might help you to get started." • The student is saying a word incorrectly and the teacher says, "When two vowels go walking, . . ." • When the student has difficulty starting to develop a writing outline, the teacher says, "I'm thinking about the mnemonic we've used for organizing an explanatory article."
Reflective	Promotion of metacognition—getting the student to think about their thinking—so that the student can use the resulting insight to determine next steps or the solution to a problem	• The student has just produced a solution incorrectly, and the teacher says, "Does that make sense? Think about the numbers you are working with and the meaning of the operation." • A teacher says, "I see you're thinking strategically. What would be the next logical step?" • When the student fails to include evidence in their writing, the teacher says, "What are we learning today? What was our purpose?"

Figure 7.5 (Continued)

Type of Prompt	Definition	Example
Heuristic	Engagement in an informal, self-directed problem-solving procedure The approach the student comes up with does not have to be like anyone else's approach, but it does need to work.	• When the student does not get the correct answer to a math problem, the teacher says, "Maybe drawing a visual representation would help you see the problem." • When the student has difficulty explaining the relationships between characters in a text, the teacher says, "Maybe drawing a visual representation of the main character's connections to one another will help you." • When a student gets stuck and cannot think of what to write next the teacher says, "Writers have a lot of different ways for getting unstuck. Some just write whatever comes to mind, others create a visual, others talk it out with a reader, and others take a break and walk around for a few minutes. Will any of those help you?" • A teacher says, "Do you think you might find it easier to begin with a simpler but similar problem? What might that problem look like?"

Source: Adapted from Fisher, D., & Frey, N. (2014). *Better learning through structured teaching: A framework for the gradual release of responsibility* (2nd ed.). Alexandria, VA: ASCD.

Figure 7.6 Types of Cues

Type of Cue	Definition	Example
Visual	A range of graphic hints that guide students through thinking or understanding	• Highlighting places on a text where students have made errors • Creating a graphic organizer to arrange content visually • Asking students to take a second look at a graphic or visual from a textbook
Verbal	Variations in speech used to draw attention to something specific or verbal attention getters that focus students' thinking	• "This is important: _____." • "This is the tricky part. Be careful and be sure to _____." • Repeating a student's statement using a questioning intonation • Changing volume or speed of speech for emphasis
Gestural	Teacher's body movements or motions used to draw attention to something that has been missed	• Making a hand motion that has been taught in advance such as one used to indicate the importance of summarizing or predicting while reading • Placing thumbs around a key idea in a text that the student was missing
Environmental	Using the surroundings, and things in the surroundings, to influence students' understanding	• Using algebra tiles, magnetic letters, or other manipulatives to guide students' thinking • Moving an object or person so that the orientation changes and guides thinking

Source: Adapted from Fisher, D., & Frey, N. (2013). *Better learning through structured teaching: A framework for the gradual release of responsibility* (2nd ed.). Alexandria, VA: ASCD.

In addition to lessons that rely on questions, prompts, and cues to address errors and misconceptions, there are times when teachers meet with groups of students for coaching. In this case, teachers meet with a small group of students, based on their identified learning needs, and provide instruction. For example, a group of students in Maria Sandoval's English class did not provide evidence in their writing. She met with them online to provide coaching about this necessary part of the task.

In other cases, these sessions are less focused on the specific academic content that students need to learn and are more focused on social skills, communication skills, or interpersonal skills. For example, Angela Jung noticed that some of her students were not reaching consensus about the ideas in the text they were reading. She took notes while watching their video and scheduled a time to meet with them. As part of the coaching session, she provided the students with a recorded example from other group (with their permission) and asked what they noticed from observing these other students.

"They listen better than we do," Adam said.

Toby added, "Yeah, and they talk one at a time. Also, they were able to get the work done pretty fast. We take forever and it's not always really good when we're done."

"I like how they compromised," Sarah said. "They got to a good place and they could all support it."

"What do you think you could try so that your group meetings are more productive?" Ms. Jung asked.

The students shared ideas and Ms. Jung made a list. After several minutes, she shared her screen, adding, "I think that this summarizes your ideas. Can you take a minute and review my notes so we can revise or add to it?"

The students did and their conversation continued. Over time, they reached agreement and committed to try out their new plans. They each took a picture of the screen and promised to have that open the next time they met. At the end of their meeting, Ms. Jung said, "I hope you are proud of yourselves and I look forward to your future conversations. These are really good skills to build; they're important in a lot of contexts."

Later, reflecting on the experience, Ms. Jung said, "The interesting thing about distance learning is time. Some groups need a lot more time and other need less time. In my physical classroom, everyone has to stop at the same time so that we can go on with the lesson. In distance learning, if a group take two hours to reach consensus and develop their product, it's totally fine. The point is that they're learning."

PRACTICING

Nick Regas talks about the importance of practice in learning.

The final aspect of our instructional model focuses on practice. And students need a lot of practice. One might even suggest overpracticing if they are going to learn something and then be able to apply it. Consider reading. Yes, children need to be taught to read. But if they never practice it, the instruction is not likely to stick. The same is true for all of the other things that students need to learn. Can you imagine never practicing the guitar, Spanish, or baseball and yet still expect to excel at it? Not likely to happen. Students need to engage in practice as part of their distance learning experiences.

One of the findings related to practice in the Visible Learning database is that *spaced practice* is much more effective than *mass practice*. In fact, the effect size of spaced practice is 0.65. The implication for distance learning (not to mention face-to-face classes) is that students should cycle through practice experiences across time. Rather than assign fifteen odd-numbered problems on a given day, space them out. And include problems from the past so that students still have to apply their knowledge to those types of challenges. It's better to have students practice thirty minutes each day rather than 2.5 hours on Friday.

In addition, *deliberate practice* is important. The effect size is 0.79. We recognize that "practice" is often equated with "mindless repetitions," which is counter to deliberate practice. To get the effect size of 0.79, students must focus their attention and engage in the tasks with the specific goal of improving performance, and there needs to be feedback that helps students know where best to move next in their learning. Goals are important. For example, the effect size of appropriately challenging goals is 0.50. Having learning goals versus not having them has an effect size of 0.51. And committing to a goal has an effect size of 0.40. Key to this is that students have a mastery goal orientation rather than a performance goal orientation. In other words, it's more valuable to say, "I want to learn to write well" or "I want to use my writing to create changes in the world" than to say, "I want to get an A on this essay" or "I want to pass this class." When students have goals, they are more likely to engage in deliberate practice.

One of the key aspects of *deliberate practice* is the development of a mental representation. A mental representation is like a really well-developed mental model of how the world should work. As Ericsson and Pool (2016) noted, mental representations are "preexisting patterns of information—facts, images, rules relationships, and so on—that are held in long-term memory and that can be used to respond quickly and effectively in certain types of situations. The thing that all mental representations have in common is that they make it possible to process large amounts of information quickly, despite the limitations of short-term memory" (pp. 65–66). If students have no idea what it means to have learned something—returning back to the idea of success criteria presented in Module 5—it will be very difficult for them to develop a mental representation and thus cannot engage in deliberate practice. In other words, practice is more effective when students know why they are doing it, have a mastery goal orientation, and understand what success looks like.

STUDENTS NEED A LOT OF PRACTICE. ONE MIGHT EVEN SUGGEST OVERPRACTICING IF THEY ARE GOING TO LEARN SOMETHING AND THEN BE ABLE TO APPLY IT.

NOTE TO SELF

How can I design practice experiences for my students?

Spaced

Deliberate

CONCLUSION

Nick Swift talks about the role of practice in his online career and technical education class.

Designing learning experiences for students is an important aspect of every educator's job. There are any number of strategies that might work to improve students' learning. We hope that you select ones that have some evidence that they are likely to be effective. And we hope that you will monitor your students' learning and make adjustments if they are not making progress. We presented a range of instructional routines organized into an instructional framework that includes demonstrating, coaching and facilitating, collaborating, and practicing. As a final task for this module, now that you have considered instructional design for distance learning, complete the following self-assessment.

FACTOR	USING THE "TRAFFIC LIGHT" SCALE, EVALUATE YOUR CURRENT LEVEL OF IMPLEMENTATION (GREEN IS GOOD OR REGULARLY; RED IS THE OPPOSITE).	USING THE SCALE BELOW, DETERMINE HOW IMPORTANT THIS FACTOR IS FOR YOU.
Demonstrating		not at all somewhat very extremely
Collaborating		not at all somewhat very extremely
Coaching and facilitating		not at all somewhat very extremely
Practicing		not at all somewhat very extremely

SUCCESS CRITERIA

- I can identify high-leverage instructional strategies that are likely to impact students' learning.

- I can adjust instructional experiences when students are not learning.

- I can demonstrate necessary aspects of learning for students.

- I can design collaborative tasks that are appropriately challenging.

- I can coach and facilitate students' learning based on the needs I have identified.

- I can design practice that is both spaced and deliberate.

MODULE 8

FEEDBACK, ASSESSMENT, AND GRADING

LEARNING INTENTIONS

- I am learning about feedback and its applications in distance learning.

- I am learning about the relationship between feedback and formative evaluation.

- I am learning about unique considerations distance learning poses to summative evaluation.

- I am learning about competency-based grading.

The link between feedback and assessment is a strong one. Assessment drives feedback, as evidenced each time a teacher checks for understanding and responds to what has been observed. Even better, assessments used formatively shape feedback and instruction as the teacher determines what needs to be learned next in the face of what has been and what has not yet been learned. Feedback drives learning, as the student utilizes the feedback to improve performance. Grades are derived from performance on assessments that are used summatively.

Assessment is assessment. Any assessment can be used formatively or summatively. In other words, there's nothing magical in the tool itself; it's what you do with it (or don't do with teaching practices). It has the potential to be eye-opening—to help us consider what worked and what didn't as we carefully examine the evidence of student progress. Unfortunately, it has more often been used as an isolated measure of a given student's achievement at one point in time than it has as a nuanced consideration of the overall trajectory of their learning experience. Feedback is the connective tissue in the assessment system. It serves as a way to drive learning in the moment and when the learning is measured cumulatively. Grades give further feedback to the student as a measure of mastery.

High school statistics teacher Matt Alexander describes these as "links in a paper chain." His students at times are in a face-to-face classroom, while at other points in the year they have been in virtual classrooms. "The learning has to continue, regardless of where it's occurring. There are some adjustments that I make depending on the setting. What I've done is shift my feedback processes so that there's more continuity in either setting."

He used the example of a recent experiment his students completed online. Mr. Alexander explained that they had been studying principles of the Stroop effect, which holds that incongruent stimuli affects response time. You've probably seen this. Color names are written on flashcards in either the correct color font, or an incorrect one. Thus, the word "green" is sometimes written in a green font (congruent) or in in a yellow font (incongruent). His students took an online Stroop test and entered their completion times and percentage of accuracy on a collaborative document. Later the same week, students used the data to draw conclusions in a formal lab report.

"As I read each student's results, I recorded a short video to provide them with in-the-moment feedback," he said. "I also noticed there was a pattern to an error in building their scatterplots I was seeing. So I also recorded a new lesson for them to watch in which I revisited outliers, direction, form, and strength. Students who needed to redid their lab report and resubmitted," he recalled. "In the past, it would have been difficult for them to get their heads wrapped around the idea of revising and resubmitting. But we've made this a core process whether we are face-to-face or in distance learning. And I'm giving them feedback and recorded lessons on our learning management system whether we're physically together or not. It makes shifting between mediums a lot simpler."

The shift to distance learning has raised questions about how feedback, assessment, and grading might be affected in virtual environments. As with previous modules, we ask you to leverage what you already know about this subject in your face-to-face classroom experiences. Take a few minutes to identify your goals for each and how you know you are achieving these goals. You'll revisit these goals at the end of the module.

DRAWING ON MY EXPERTISE

What are your goals for each? How do you assess whether you have achieved these goals?

	GOALS	EVIDENCE OF SUCCESS TOWARD GOALS
Feedback to students	• _____ • _____ • _____ • _____ • _____	• _____ • _____ • _____ • _____ • _____
Formative evaluation	• _____ • _____ • _____ • _____ • _____	• _____ • _____ • _____ • _____ • _____
Summative evaluation	• _____ • _____ • _____ • _____ • _____	• _____ • _____ • _____ • _____ • _____
Grading	• _____ • _____ • _____ • _____ • _____	• _____ • _____ • _____ • _____ • _____

 Available for download at **resources.corwin.com/distancelearningplaybook**

FEEDBACK TO STUDENTS

ASSESSMENTS USED FORMATIVELY SHAPE FEEDBACK AND INSTRUCTION.

Feedback has been described as the most underutilized instructional approach we teachers have at our disposal. Teachers will often say that they know feedback is useful, but they offer *useful* feedback surprisingly infrequently, with most incidents consisting of general praise of a nonspecific nature ("You've done a fantastic job!"), and usually only one or two sentences in length (Voerman, Meijer, Korthagen, & Simons, 2012). It truly is a lost opportunity as well, since the effect size of feedback is 0.66 and likely to have a positive impact on student learning (Hattie, 2018). The purpose of feedback should remain constant—to progressively close the gap between present and desired performance (Hattie & Timperley, 2007).

But the usefulness of feedback varies considerably. Corrective feedback alone isn't especially effective for anything other than new learning. For example, corrective feedback during a flashcard game with a young child who is just learning numerals is useful ("No, that's a number 8, not a 6."). But much of the feedback provided to students concerns their application of knowledge. Telling a student, "Your answer to this word problem is wrong—the answer is 24," is less effective, because it doesn't provide any additional information about the processes he used or the path forward.

More effective is the use of high-information feedback that consists of corrective feedback coupled with information about processes and self-regulation (Wisniewski, Zierer, & Hattie, 2020). These dense feedback units address the three major questions learners have:

- Where am I going?
- How am I going there?
- Where will I go next?

Chris Ewing talks about the purpose and types of feedback students need in distance learning.

WHERE AM I GOING?

The first question is addressed through the learning intentions and success criteria. Knowing what success looks like allows students to work toward their learning goals. Feedback can be used to ensure students information about their approximation of the learning. For example, sixth-grade social studies teacher Kika Garcia recorded voice feedback on a student's online draft informational essay about rise of the samurai warrior caste in twelfth-century Japan. She began by saying, "*You provided an account of the event at the beginning of the paper which sets the context for the reader. What's missing so far is information about earlier events that foreshadowed what happened.*"

HOW AM I GOING THERE?

The second question concerns the use of strategies that might address the discrepancies between execution and success. Ms. Garcia added, "*So let's talk for a few minutes about where you might locate this information. Making a list of sources to check out is going to prevent you from forgetting the ideas we brainstorm.*"

WHERE WILL I GO NEXT?

The third question is answered when the teacher shifts the focus to the student's future actions. The social studies teacher continued, "*What's next for you? It's important that you have a plan. What are two or three things you're going to do?*" Feedback, as Brookhart (2008) describes it, needs to be "just-in-time, just-for-me information delivered when and where it can do the most good" (p. 1).

Elleisha Elzein talks about providing feedback to students.

THE SOCIOEMOTIONAL LINKS TO FEEDBACK

When students are engaged in appropriately challenging tasks, they are more likely to respond to feedback because they need that information to continue growing and learning. Feedback focused on something that you already know does little to change understanding. And feedback thrives on errors. When errors are celebrated and expected, feedback can gain a foothold. The relationship between the person providing the feedback and the person receiving it has a mediating effect on the usefulness of the feedback. But it's only when the feedback is received that it works. Consider the complex dimensions that are required to accomplish this:

- The relationship between the teacher and student needs to be a positive one.

- The teacher needs to be seen as credible in the eyes of the student.

- The climate of the classroom needs to be such that errors are not viewed with shame, but as part of the learning process.

CORRECTIVE FEEDBACK ALONE ISN'T ESPECIALLY EFFECTIVE FOR ANYTHING OTHER THAN NEW LEARNING.

In a study of middle and high school students' attitudes about feedback on their writing, Zumbrunn and her colleagues (2016) found that 20 percent of them disregarded it because they didn't have a good relationship with their teachers. While the study didn't explore the nature of these relationships, it seems apparent that the feedback required effort on the part of the teacher. It

Select a well-designed student task you have used before (see Module 6 for a refresher on engaging tasks). What do you need to do to provide high-information feedback?

"Where am I going?"

Success criteria

"How am I going there?"

Feedback about processes

"Where will I go next?"

Self-regulatory feedback

 Available for download at **resources.corwin.com/distancelearningplaybook**

is discouraging to think that one out of five students might theoretically reject it out of hand.

Something we wonder about is whether in some cases the feedback is misplaced. It doesn't work across the board for all situations. In fact, in their meta-analyses on feedback, Wisniewski, Zierer, and Hattie (2020) report that "feedback has higher impact on cognitive and motor skills outcomes than on motivational and behavioral outcomes" (p. 1). Yet how often is feedback used in a misguided attempt to motivate or change behavior? Confine your feedback to the more effective realms of cognitive and motor skills, while remaining cognizant of the social and emotional conditions required to make your feedback useful.

Ebony Peralta talks about the relationship between student–teacher relationships and feedback.

A VIEW FROM THE EARLY YEARS

Most early learning assessment is administered in natural settings through teacher observations. Many programs use a developmental continuum along which a child's observed behavior is assessed. During any given day, a child may call out some version of "Look at me!" more than a dozen times. They want it recorded—a timestamp, a video, a photo. We are present and ready to provide a powerful interaction. Our early learning team is aware of the range of knowledge and skills our children develop when they interact with grown-ups and other children. We know the gains are greater with others than alone. We include feedback that says, "I see you . . ." or "You're on the right track!" Effective feedback is peppered with praise, a probe, an action step, practice, planning and follow up. We use these six steps with our children and adult learners.

Using interactive journals is a splendid way to ask and answer questions and provide feedback. In an early learning classroom of twenty, it is easy to read and respond to five journals each night. I send a Flipgrid question for children to answer. They record their response on Flipgrid (the recording helps me decipher their writing) and show it to me in their actual paper journal. I respond and send a new question based on what they wrote. The next day, I read and respond to five more journals. As the year progresses, their questions back to me are more detailed, their grammar improved in their spoken language, their details, richer. My students gain practice using pronouns and possessive 's.' In June, no one is saying, "I went to my Grandma house."

We are continuing with student-led conferences. The expectation was the meeting would be held every quarter for forty-five minutes, resulting in a contract that spelled out attainable goals for each party. The children showed and explained their best work, what they needed to bolster their efforts, and included what was holding them back. The child set goals for themselves. They listed what they needed from their family and what I could do to help. This kind of focused commitment has garnered remarkable results. We're continuing to do this with the children and their families in virtual meetings.

By Claudia Readwright

In what ways do you foster social and emotional elements of learning to leverage feedback? What errors do you want to avoid?

	WAYS YOU FOSTER	ERRORS TO AVOID
Teacher–student relationships		
Teacher credibility		
Classroom climate that accepts errors		

 Available for download at **resources.corwin.com/distancelearningplaybook**

FEEDBACK AT A DISTANCE

Technology offers great possibilities when it comes to distance learning. The highest effects of digital technology are interactive videos (0.54) and intelligent tutoring systems (0.51).

Interactive videos, whether teacher made or commercially produced, require students to respond to questions interspersed throughout. Practices like this are commonly done in face-to-face teaching, such as using interactive read alouds that are punctuated with questions intended to foster comprehension. However, interactive videos offer a superior advantage that can't be fully replicated in live teaching: The student can view it again and again. This reduces the cognitive overload students might otherwise experience because they can rewatch segments that are more difficult. In addition, interactive videos are associated with increased attention and greater reflection, likely due to increased student choice and control. As one example, you can rewatch the video of Angie Hackman in Module 7 as she uses a video she created on an interactive video platform. This platform brings a student who has answered incorrectly back to the segment of the video that is pertinent to the question so that the student can view it again.

Intelligent tutoring systems (ITS) are commercially produced and mirror many of the best features of feedback. Information is presented and the system asks questions, provides feedback or hints, and gives prompts. Based on the student's responses, the system adapts questions, feedback, and prompts (Ma, Adesope, Nesbit, & Liu, 2014). Examples of ITS programs include AutoTutor, Cognitive Tutor, and ALEKS. It should be noted that ITS programs are not "plug and play" and require investment in professional learning for teachers.

Easier to implement are feedback mechanisms that capitalize on your knowledge of the students and your relationship with them. The Read&Write function on Google Docs allows you to highlight a portion of a student's submitted work and record a voice comment for feedback. As noted in Module 3, voice-recorded comments give you the opportunity to use students' names and give them the chance to hear the warmth and tone behind the feedback. Unlike a written comment, which is a bit more decontextualized, a recorded comment comes closer to simulating the kind of verbal feedback you would offer in a face-to-face setting. These voice notes offer another important opportunity, as students can also record questions and comments for the teacher.

Feedback from the student to the teacher is especially important in distance learning. Be sure to

- Solicit feedback from students regularly to find out how they are experiencing their online learning.

THE RELATIONSHIP BETWEEN THE PERSON PROVIDING THE FEEDBACK AND THE PERSON RECEIVING IT HAS A MEDIATING EFFECT ON THE USEFULNESS OF THE FEEDBACK. BUT IT'S ONLY WHEN THE FEEDBACK IS RECEIVED THAT IT WORKS.

- Ask them about the videos and materials you have been preparing for them and whether they find them useful, or whether they are using them at all.

- Find out about their own self-regulation by asking them to reflect on the previous week and note whether they asked a question of the teacher outside of the live session.

Jeff Bonine talks about feedback from students.

Couple this with the user analytics you can gather on how often various materials and videos were accessed on your learning management system (LMS) to gather data in real time. The feedback gained from students gives you direction about what to continue, what to do more of, and what isn't especially useful to them.

NOTE TO SELF

What special considerations do you need to keep in mind when providing feedback to students in a virtual environment? How will you solicit feedback from students?

FORMATIVE EVALUATION

Dylan Wiliam makes a crucial point when he says, as David Ausubel noted more than 50 years ago, "good teaching starts from where the learner is, rather than where we would like her or him to be" (Wiliam, 2020). The practice of formative evaluation requires that teachers check for understanding throughout lessons, not only at the end. The practice of formative evaluation with students has been shown to be of benefit to teachers in making decisions about next steps in teaching, as measured by gains in student learning. With an effect size of 0.34, it is likely to have a positive impact on student learning. However, the power of formative evaluation doesn't reside solely in the act of administering the quiz or assignment. It is the feedback from the assessment, not the assessment itself, that matters. Its power is amplified when (1) the student and the teacher understand the results and (2) the teacher and the student use the results to take action on future teaching and learning. In other words, formative evaluation shouldn't be done only so the teacher can make decisions (that's important) but also so the student can make decisions.

There are a number of ways to check for understanding, such as exit slips, story retellings, poll responses to questions, and practice quizzes. A virtual environment allows for all of these to occur, albeit in ways that may differ from methods used in a face-to-face classroom.

VIRTUAL EXIT SLIPS

Provide students with a range of possible responses and ask them to use the options at the end of assignments or virtual class sessions. Fifth-grade teacher Kyle Davidson asks his students to gauge their level of understanding at the end of each mathematics assignment. His students are given four possible responses to choose from:

1. I'm just learning (I need more help).

2. I'm almost there (I need more practice).

3. I own it! (I can work independently).

4. I'm a pro! (I can teach others).

Mr. Davidson said, "I get their feedback about where they think they are, and that helps me plan for some specialized support. Once a week, I schedule a live session and divide them up based on their feedback. I manually populate breakout rooms with those students who have ranked themselves as a 2 or a 3 so they can support one another." Those students who feel like they can teach others are generally smaller in number, "so I distribute them carefully in breakout rooms that might need some additional expertise," said Mr. Davidson.

Annaleah Gonzalez talks about checking for understanding in her distance learning classes.

He chooses tasks for these breakout rooms that are culled from the week's assignments that proved to be more challenging. "So, I give them ten minutes or so to work through a parallel problem together."

In the meantime, the teacher is meeting up with his small group of students who had asked for more help. "It's a chance for me to reteach and find out where their barriers lie. If I need more time with individual students, I schedule an additional session just for them." He calls this portion of his online class Mastery Monday so that his students always know when to expect this routine. "The whole thing only takes about fifteen minutes, but it is a great warm-up for all of us. When we return to the main room, it becomes our first whole-class discussion. I ask them, "What are you learning about yourself as a learner?" because I want to reinforce the value in persistence and collaborative problem solving in mathematics."

VOICE-RECORDED COMMENTS GIVE YOU THE OPPORTUNITY TO USE STUDENTS' NAMES AND GIVE THEM THE CHANCE TO HEAR THE WARMTH AND TONE BEHIND THE FEEDBACK.

VIRTUAL RETELLINGS

Retellings are used with elementary students for a variety of purposes, including fostering listening comprehension, oral composition, sequencing ability, attention, and memory. For younger children, retellings allow teachers to determine whether a child can process language when the burden of reading a text is removed. One of the easiest ways to do this is to read a short text to a student and then invite them to retell the story.

First-grade teacher Nur Shihab records her read alouds for her students and posts them on her LMS. "The students like being able to listen to them again and again, judging by the number of replays I can see on the LMS teacher dashboard," she said. Each week, she selects three or four students to record a retelling of a story she has selected. "I notify the family that I'll be doing this, as there's usually some assistance from an adult at home to manage the recording," said Ms. Shihab. "I've found it's actually really helpful to have a recorded retelling, because I can replay it, too." She continued, "My grade level uses rubrics for retelling informational and narrative texts. I use those to assess each child and monitor their progress." Ms. Shihab added one other unexpected benefit. "When I schedule parent–teacher conferences, I can show the family comparative recordings from early in the school year and more currently. Families really get to see the progress their child is making."

POLLING TO RESPOND TO QUESTIONS

Teachers have increasingly used polls to solicit information from students in face-to-face environments, and they prove to be even more useful in distance learning environments. As one example, virtual staff meetings at the school where two of us work regularly include Kahoot! questions (a game-based learning platform) about school improvement and professional learning topics. Teachers respond on their cell phones to multiple choice questions, and a bar graph populates on the shared screen to gauge the number of correct and incorrect responses. Similar polling functions are often built in to learning management systems and provide feedback to the teacher in real time about the current status of student learning.

PRACTICE TESTS

Formative practice testing, in which students take short quizzes to understand their command of the subject or topic, is an effective way to check for understanding while also prompting deliberative practice. These formative practice tests are low stakes and not part of the student's grade, as the emphasis here is on practice to gain self-knowledge of learning gaps. A meta-analysis of the effectiveness of formative practice testing on advancing student learning reported these findings (Adesope, Trevisan, & Sundararajan, 2017):

- Lots of practice tests didn't increase student learning. Once is often enough.

- Feedback paired with the practice test enhances learning.

- Their usefulness was strong at both the elementary and secondary levels.

- The value of formative practice tests is in students reflecting on their results.

Jonathon Walker talks about the use of practice tests.

Biology teacher Marcus Lopez uses short practice tests with his students asynchronously, then scores them and uses the results to drive a subsequent live virtual session. His students have been learning about diffusion and osmosis. Mr. Lopez previously posed questions for his students to respond to, so that he and they could gauge their understanding of the topic. After taking a five-question audience response quiz at the midpoint in the unit, the students in his class analyzed their results and then met in breakout rooms aligned to the questions. "I join each group for a few minutes so I can listen in on conversations. They've gotten very used to me popping in and out," said the teacher.

"GOOD TEACHING STARTS FROM WHERE THE LEARNER IS, RATHER THAN WHERE WE WOULD LIKE HER OR HIM TO BE."

Gabriella did not answer two of the questions correctly, but was especially puzzled by the fourth question, which asked about osmotic pressure. Gabriella chose to meet with a group of students who had selected the same question so that they could build on each other's knowledge. Gabriella and several other students did a search of their biology textbook and reread the background information about it. "Oh, I remember this now!" she said. Luke, another member of the group, replayed the osmotic pressure lab they had watched the previous week. "There was more sugar in one solution than the other, and when there was a semi-permeable membrane between them. . . ." Gabriela finished, "The sugar concentration balanced." She later remarked, "When I watched that lab it went right past me. I like the practice quizzes Mr. Lopez gives because it helps me see things I didn't notice the first time. It gives me an idea about where my practice needs to be to get reading for the end-of-unit test." This example helps highlight that via distance learning students often have the chance to replay lecture video many times, an opportunity often denied in the regular classroom.

How do you check for understanding in your distance learning classes? Below, add other methods you are using or intend to use to check for understanding formatively and summatively.

	USEFUL AND CURRENTLY USING IT	USEFUL AND HAVEN'T USED IT YET	NOT USEFUL FOR MY CLASS
Virtual Exit Slips			
Virtual Retellings			
Polling and Audience Response Methods			
Practice Tests			

online resources — Available for download at **resources.corwin.com/distancelearningplaybook**

SUMMATIVE EVALUATIONS

Summative evaluations typically come at the end of a unit of instruction. Such assessments test cumulative knowledge and skills learned at the end of a unit of work, over a semester, or at the end of a course. The design of these vary widely depending on students' developmental needs and the nature of the topic or course. A distance learning environment prompts additional concerns about testing security, given that a teacher's usual ability to proctor an exam in a face-to-face classroom is limited when it must be completed virtually. Having acknowledged that, here are some considerations for promoting authenticity in summative evaluations.

- **Become acquainted with your LMS assessment tools.** Your learning platform likely includes features that allow for a specific timed testing window, as well as a randomization feature that allows items to appear in a unique order for each student.

- **Proctor shorter exams in live sessions.** Use a timed live session and have students turn their cameras on so that you can observe them during the test.

- **Use text-matching software for essays.** Many school systems use plagiarism detection programs as part of their online learning. Even in face-to-face settings, these are valuable teaching tools. That's key—teach students about the use of text-matching tools and don't misuse them as a way to catch them doing something wrong.

- **Expand your repertoire of assessment formats.** Oral tests have long been viewed as a useful option for some students, but the amount of time teachers have in face-to-face classrooms has limited their use to a smaller number of students. But in a distance learning classroom, students can record themselves presenting their summaries of their learning for the teacher to view individually.

- **Teach students about academic honesty and ethical decision-making.** Take a proactive approach by embedding these topics into classroom discourse. A statement of academic honesty should be introduced in the first weeks of school and featured prominently on your LMS and at the beginning of each assessment. At the school where two of us work, it has been the practice for several years that students sign an academic honesty statement as part of each summative assessment. Most of all, infuse discussions about ethical decision-making—a key socioemotional learning skill—into your subject area when testing is not a primary focus.

FORMATIVE EVALUATION SHOULDN'T BE DONE ONLY SO THE TEACHER CAN MAKE DECISIONS (THAT'S IMPORTANT) BUT ALSO SO THE STUDENT CAN MAKE DECISIONS.

This is not an exhaustive list of ways to check for understanding through summative evaluation. On the next page, we invite you to consider approaches we have highlighted and to add your own to your menu of options for checking for understanding.

What tools does my LMS offer?	
How can I proctor assessments?	
What text-matching systems can I use?	
What assessment formats can I use?	
What do I need to teach students in relation to academic honesty and ethical decision-making in distance learning?	

COMPETENCY-BASED GRADING

Most teachers will tell you that grades are given to reflect a student's mastery of a concept or subject, but upon looking deeper, you discover that several other nonacademic factors are in the formula. Let's take a fictional student and call him Bob. Did he bring materials to class? Check. Did he turn in his homework? Sometimes. Did he behave reasonably well in class? Nope. So what's his grade for the course? Naturally, you would say that this isn't enough information and you need to know what his summative evaluations looked like. Yet too often organization, compliance, and behavior are lumped in with evaluations of learning. This is not to say that these nonacademic indicators are unimportant, but rather that when factored in with learning performance they obscure the signal. And in this model, things quickly turn personal and undermine the relationship between the teacher and the learner. Instead of being able to tie his academic performance to his world history grade, Bob grumbles, "My teacher doesn't like me. He's always on my case. That's why I'm failing." The resentment builds, Bob only gets more sullen, and now his teacher really doesn't like him. Bob's learning trajectory looks increasingly dismal, and in the meantime, he continues to externalize as he blames others.

In an effort to end negative and ultimately futile cycles like this, more schools are turning to competency-based grading systems across face-to-face and distance learning settings. This system focuses on mastery of content and eliminates grading of practice work and nonacademic behaviors. The school where Doug and Nancy work has employed this system for more than a decade (Fisher, Frey, & Pumpian, 2011). Students receive grades based on their performance on summative evaluations only, typically between four and six per quarter. Assignments and homework are regarded as formative evaluation for both the teacher and the student, and do not earn points toward the course grade. Of course, some students don't do the homework (they are teenagers). However, in time most learn the value of the practice that allows them to master the content.

The switch to distance learning has been made a bit easier at our school because this model was already in place. Because the learning week looks different than in a brick-and-mortar school, units of instruction are often organized as online modules that combine synchronous and asynchronous learning experiences. Students are encountering more self-paced and self-directed learning, and teachers are finding themselves relying less on in-class assignments and other small tasks. Competency-based grading has the added benefit of avoiding the error of averaging multiple tasks. Imagine if the written and performance portions of a driving test were averaged such that a failing score on one but an exemplary score on the other would result in a driver's license. Few of us would be in favor of sharing the road with someone who had either failed at operating the vehicle properly or was not knowledgeable about traffic laws.

Ricki Wilder talks about competency-based assessment.

THE VALUE OF FORMATIVE PRACTICE TESTS IS IN STUDENTS REFLECTING ON THEIR RESULTS.

Students in the competency-based grading model used at our high school are required to pass each summative evaluation (usually a test, essay, or other complex performance task) at a level of 70 percent or higher. Students who do not meet this threshold receive an Incomplete, signaling to them and their family that mastery has not yet been attained. These learners are required to attend virtual tutorials and must complete the homework packet (whether for the first time or again) before taking another version of the exam. A decade of observation of a few thousand middle and high school students has led us to these conclusions:

- With time, most students learn the value of their active participation in their learning.

- Relationships between teachers and students are healthier because much of the subjective nature of grading has been removed.

- It's really hard to implement and requires revisiting these policies regularly to revise and improve them.

Among the changes we have made over the years are these:

- Adding a separate but robust citizenship grade that accompanies each academic grade

- Strengthening midterms and finals to include cumulative knowledge for the semester

- Improving family conferences to marshal home supports

- Confronting students with carried incompletes at a distance learning summer school

TOO OFTEN ORGANIZATION, COMPLIANCE, AND BEHAVIOR ARE LUMPED IN WITH EVALUATIONS OF LEARNING.

Rather than offer six-week credit recovery courses, it's the Incompletes that must be addressed. Therefore, summer school may take four days for some students and longer for others. Historically, we seem to have more summer school Incompletes with younger students compared to older ones, which may be an indication of developing self-regulatory skills. By no means do we suggest that in practice a competency-based grading system is clean and easy. It's messy and hard. But we hope that our students gain a deeper understanding of themselves as learners and what they need to do next to be successful. We are discovering that these dispositions are becoming even more crucial when students are in a distance learning environment.

You may or may not be ready to think about competency-based grading at this time. But we do hope that grading is a part of your discussions with colleagues, even if the decision is to hold steady with your current grading system. Effective educators are willing to revisit procedures and policies in order to promote learning. Your willingness to have the discussion is evidence of the first mindframe: "*I focus on learning and the language of learning.*"

NOTE TO SELF

Use these questions to spark discussion about grading practices in the context of distance learning.

What is working well for us as it pertains to grading in distance learning?

What problems are we encountering in using our current grading system in a distance learning environment?

What successful distance learning grading practices are we aware of?

How might we investigate other successful distance learning grading practices?

 Available for download at **resources.corwin.com/distancelearningplaybook**

CONCLUSION

Formative and summative evaluation play an essential role in signaling learning progress to students, especially when they are actively engaged in viewing data, making strategic decisions, and taking action on next steps. These evaluative processes bracket the high-information feedback provided to students. These practices are even more important in a distance learning environment. Take a few minutes to revisit the goals you identified for feedback, formative evaluation, summative evaluation, and grading. Then assess yourself on the factors discussed in this module.

FACTOR	USING THE "TRAFFIC LIGHT" SCALE, EVALUATE YOUR CURRENT LEVEL OF IMPLEMENTATION (GREEN IS GOOD OR REGULARLY; RED IS THE OPPOSITE).	USING THE SCALE BELOW, DETERMINE HOW IMPORTANT THIS FACTOR IS FOR YOU.
Feedback to students		not at all somewhat very extremely
The socioemotional links to feedback		not at all somewhat very extremely
Feedback at a distance		not at all somewhat very extremely
Formative evaluation		not at all somewhat very extremely
Summative evaluation		not at all somewhat very extremely
Competency-based grading		not at all somewhat very extremely

SUCCESS CRITERIA

- I can tailor my feedback procedures to a distance learning environment.

- I can enhance feedback using principles of socioemotional learning.

- I can identify formative evaluation techniques to check for understanding in virtual settings.

- I can identify features on my learning management system that enhance summative evaluation experiences.

- I can determine the feasibility and authenticity of my current grading procedures in a distance learning setting.

MODULE 9

LEARNING, DISTANCE OR OTHERWISE

LEARNING INTENTIONS

- I am learning to consider experiences with distance learning as a way to bring schools back better than before.

- I am learning about the ways to improve the schooling experience, whether distance, blended, or physically together.

Chas Beam talks about the importance of social and emotional learning.

Schooling underwent radical change worldwide in the spring of 2020. Due to a global pandemic, learners of all ages suddenly found themselves attempting to navigate unfamiliar technologies in settings that had not previously been used as dedicated learning spaces (bedrooms, kitchen tables, and garages, to name a few). Teachers and school leaders heroically shifted instruction from face-to-face classrooms to virtual ones seemingly overnight. Districts and states mobilized to get technology and WiFi access into the hands of families who needed it. Teachers learned to work from home, while juggling all of the additional challenges of managing children, pets, roommates, and partners. These emergency efforts focused primarily on converting what had been occurring in brick and mortar classrooms to digital ones. There was no time to plan for this. We were in crisis mode. During that time, we learned some important lessons:

- Social and emotional elements of learning are interwoven with academic ones.

- Partnerships with families are central, not peripheral, to education (for teachers and students).

- Ineffective approaches to learning are ineffective in digital spaces, too.

While the scale of this rapid move to online learning was unprecedented, the fact that schools were able to do so is not. Ask any educator who has taught in the immediate aftermath of Hurricane Katrina in New Orleans, the Christchurch earthquake in New Zealand, or the bush fires in Australia. You'll find dedicated educators who brought stability and optimism to the communities they serve, even as they dealt with their own devastation.

DRAWING ON MY EXPERTISE

What did you learn from crisis teaching? What will be useful in the future?

Here's what didn't happen: we didn't take advantage as a field to truly learn from these efforts about what to do *better*. The focus was on a return to normalcy, to the status quo. The moment we were able to, we turned our attention back to the familiar. There was no looking back to identify lessons learned and act upon them. Let's not do that this time. Instead, our focus should be on how to leverage what we are learning to make schooling better in face-to-face and distance learning spaces. As Sir Winston Churchill is purported to have said, "Never let a crisis go to waste." There's been a crisis. How can we make sure it doesn't go to waste?

LEARNING FROM OTHER CRISES

We know from the aftermath of Hurricane Katrina in New Orleans how important it is for teachers and school leaders to be visible, decisive, trustworthy, respected, and willing to engage in frontline work (Porche, 2009). After Katrina, those who had a prior history of problems were more likely to show symptoms of traumatic stress, depression, sadness, anger, anxiety, and loneliness—for both students and teachers (Osofsky, Osofsky, & Harris, 2007). But the effect on student achievement was not as great as many expected. Students were out of school between three and seven weeks and many had no school work in this time. There was a drop of -0.17 from Katrina, but "what is more surprising is how quickly the Parish evacuees recovered from the experience and actually began to see gains in test scores" (Sacerdote, 2012, p. 131; see also Pane, McCaffrey, Kalra, & Zhou, 2008, who showed a drop of only 0.06 in statewide test scores from the outage).

Let's recall the effects of the Christchurch earthquakes in 2011, which severely disrupted access to schools. There was a rush to online learning with a cry for special dispensations for upper high school examinations. As advisor to the Qualifications Authority that oversaw these exams, John argued that there should not be special dispensation. He based this on strike research, which showed no effects at the upper-school level, with positive effects in some cases. Sure enough, the performance of Christchurch students went up, and as schools resumed, the scores settled back down. Why? Because, during that crisis time, teachers tailored learning more to what students could NOT do, whereas often conventional school is about what teachers *think* students need, even if students can already do the tasks. During the crisis, there was more focus on triaging learning for students and the teaching commenced from some excellent diagnoses of what students could and could not do.

In the aftermath of a crisis, students look for support from a trusted adult, seek help from peers, seek ways to express their feelings, and establish some sense of routine. Many of us, adults and children, go through feelings of shock and disorganization. There will be altruistic or heroic phases and claims, and

AS SIR WINSTON CHURCHILL IS PURPORTED TO HAVE SAID, "NEVER LET A CRISIS GO TO WASTE." THERE'S BEEN A CRISIS. HOW CAN WE MAKE SURE IT DOESN'T GO TO WASTE?

Marisa Pena talks about knowing what students already know and not wasting time.

honeymoon periods of high morale and action and optimism, but some will feel angry, displaced, and lonely.

Rob Gordon is an Australian who has studied the effects on schools from bushfires and talks about the desired state of social fusion: "In this state of fusion, members identify with each other because they share the same experience; they feel strong emotional attachments because of what they have undergone together and rapidly develop a shared culture of stories, symbols, and memories" (2004). Make sure every child experiences this fusion and becomes an insider in the online classroom. That schools and classrooms already existed helps develop this bond, but now work to maintain it. Build on symbols, rituals, and identity; model connectedness; use stories and other artifacts so that when schools reopen there is a symbol, a thing, an event—a mosaic, a play, stories, collective memories of the at-home socially distancing experience.

Sheri Johnson talks about the importance of staying positive and recognizing the range of emotions we'll all experience.

USE CRISIS LEARNING TO MAKE SCHOOLS BETTER

Technologies have allowed us to maintain learning even when brick-and-mortar schools can't be used. They are increasingly instrumental to daily instruction in the classroom, albeit in two primary ways. The first is in presenting information. Rather than film strips, we can easily access professionally produced videos! The second common use of technology in the classroom is for completing independent work. Instead of boring worksheets, we can put them on a laptop and have students complete them online. If those have been the predominant digital learning experiences for students and their teachers, it's little wonder that the initial shift to online learning was bumpy.

Kurt Olson talks about the blend of learning technologies.

You are now likely working in two mediums: distance learning and face-to-face. What matters is what you do, not where you teach. Too much lecture and too many worksheets that are not tailored to students' needs but, rather, what we "think they need" is not effective in either environment. You may have had different experiences with using technologies in face-to-face classroom settings. We invite you to reflect on your experiences with using virtual spaces within your brick-and-mortar classroom. Some examples might include written and video discussion boards, flipped learning, online modules, student-generated collaborative documents, gamified learning, and microlearning. How often do you use them, and how do you gauge student success in these mediums?

MAKE LEARNING BETTER FOR STUDENTS

Let's remember to leverage what we have learned from crisis online learning to prepare ourselves and our students for more robust and authentic future learning.

- Focus on what students **know** and **don't know**. Only teach the things that they don't know. This was one of the most important lessons learned from the Christchurch earthquakes in Australia and one that should have impacted practice since then.

- Keep in mind that **there is a balance not only for students but also for teachers**. Deliver mini-classes using social media, make them clear, and provide oodles of opportunities for feedback. Make it skill based and provide exciting ways to practice, and not just project based, which can (but does not need to) lead to busy work with little learning.

- **Harness the most exciting use of technology for our current situation**: the power of social media to enhance learning. Maree Davies and her colleagues (2017) have explored asking students to use social media on learning management systems to have students send in questions and talk about what they do not know. They are more likely to do this on social media than directly to the teacher.

- **Worry more about subjects that parents are least likely to be able to help with**, like math and science, and encourage kids and parents to read, read, read, and also talk about their reading, so the story is important, the vocabulary is stretched, and then simultaneously keep teaching the skills of reading to make reading pleasurable.

- Remember, **if students get stuck, do not know what to do next, or make errors, you should not depend on the parents to know about the errors or what best to do next**. We do not want parents giving feedback in a way that ends up with them doing the work!

- Take ownership as much as possible by building in mechanisms that allow for responsive ways to **provide timely feedback**.

- **Create as many opportunities for social interaction**, not just between you and the student, but using technology for students to work, share, interact, and learn together, as you often do in the regular classroom. Learning at home need not be a lonely activity, with the only or even primary resource the parent.

TOO MANY WORKSHEETS THAT ARE NOT TAILORED TO STUDENTS' NEEDS BUT, RATHER, WHAT WE "THINK THEY NEED" IS NOT EFFECTIVE IN ANY ENVIRONMENT.

Cynthia Ramirez talks about creating social interaction opportunities.

MAKE LEARNING BETTER FOR TEACHERS

Dominique Smith shares a message for educators.

As a field, we must also look after the teachers during this time and in the future. Part of looking after teachers is in making sure that they continue to grow professionally. Teaching is an identity and an action, not just a vocation. That leaves questions whose answers will continue to evolve. How can we

- assess our impact from a distance?

- learn how we as groups of teachers can evaluate, discuss, and work together?

- discover ways to enhance the collective efficacy of all (now with the parents)?

- view this pandemic as an opportunity to learn more about how to work with students from afar, outside of our normal comfort zones of the classroom and school?

- engage with parents to realize we as educators have unique skills and expertise (and are happy to share them), and not get upset if students are not spending five or six hours every day in the belief that school at home is but a mirror of the typical school day?

Schools, no matter via what medium, can be a hub of response and recovery, a place to support emotional recovery and promote social togetherness—and this is as important as any achievement gains. It would be wonderful to use this pandemic as an opportunity to learn about learning from afar, so share stories of success of teachers and students learning from this crisis, pay particular attention to below-average students or students with special needs, discover how to develop collective efficacy among teachers and school leaders, and use this experience to learn how to best work with all students.

LET'S REMEMBER TO LEVERAGE WHAT WE HAVE LEARNED FROM CRISIS ONLINE LEARNING TO PREPARE OURSELVES AND OUR STUDENTS FOR MORE ROBUST AND AUTHENTIC FUTURE LEARNING.

CONCLUSION

The implications from Visible Learning suggest that we can plan meaningful distance learning and positively impact students. Again, that's what this book is about. As you have seen from the modules in this playbook, there is evidence about what works and we can use that evidence to ensure that our distance learning efforts mobilize what works in face-to-face and virtual environments. We invite you to engage in a final self-assessment about your learning.

FACTOR	USING THE "TRAFFIC LIGHT" SCALE, EVALUATE YOUR CURRENT LEVEL OF IMPLEMENTATION (GREEN IS GOOD OR REGULARLY; RED IS THE OPPOSITE).	USING THE SCALE BELOW, DETERMINE HOW IMPORTANT THIS FACTOR IS FOR YOU.
Learning from this crisis		not at all somewhat very extremely
Making distance learning better for students		not at all somewhat very extremely
Making distance learning better for teachers		not at all somewhat very extremely

SUCCESS CRITERIA

- I can learn from crises and improve teaching and learning.

- I can make distance learning better for students.

- I can make distance learning better for teachers.

- I can make physical school better for everyone.

APPENDIX

PLANNING TEMPLATE

COURSE:	INSTRUCTIONAL UNIT:			TIME RANGE:	

STANDARDS	TOPIC (LEARNING PROGRESSIONS)	WEEK	IN-CLASS ACTIVITIES	FORMATIVE ASSESSMENT EXTEND – REVIEW – ASSESS – RETEACH	TEXTS AND RESOURCES
		1			
		2			
		3			

Week 4: Summative Assessment Competency

Content and Academic Vocabulary

Accommodations and Modifications for Students With Disabilities

DISTANCE LEARNING LOG

STUDENT NAME:	CONTENT:	GRADE:

WEEK OF: (DATE)

THIS WEEK'S LEARNING INTENTION(S)	TASKS/ASSESSMENTS I COMPLETED

SUCCESS CRITERIA

Use the space below to rate your learning before and after each lesson.

CRITERIA	BEFORE	AFTER
I can		
I can		

REFERENCES

Adesope, O. O., Trevisan, D. A., & Sundararajan, N. (2017). Rethinking the use of tests: A meta-analysis of practice testing. *Review of Educational Research, 87*(3), 659–701.

Alter, P., & Haydon, T. (2017). Characteristics of effective classroom rules: A review of the literature. *Teacher Education & Special Education, 40*(2), 114–127.

Altermatt, E., Jovanovic, J., & Perry, M. (1998). Bias or responsivity? Sex and achievement-level effects on teachers' classroom questioning practices. *Journal of Educational Psychology, 90*(3), 516–527.

Asay, L., & Orgill, M. (2010). Analysis of essential features of inquiry found in articles published in *The Science Teacher*, 1998–2007. *Journal of Science Teacher Education, 21*(1), 57–79.

Berry, A. (2020). Disrupting to driving: Exploring upper primary teachers' perspectives on student engagement. *Teachers and Teaching.* Advance online publication. doi: 10.1080/13540602.2020.1757421

Birch, S. H., & Ladd, G. W. (1997). The teacher–child relationship and children's early school adjustment. *Journal of School Psychology, 35*(1), 61–79.

Brink, C. R. (1935). *Caddie Woodlawn*. New York, NY: Macmillan.

Brookhart, S. (2008). *How to give effective feedback to your students*. Alexandria, VA: ASCD.

Brualdi, A. (1998). *Implementing performance assessment in the classroom*. ERIC/AE Digest [ED423312]. Retrieved from https://files.eric.ed.gov/fulltext/ED423312.pdf

Cameron, C. E., Connor, C. M., & Morrison, F. J. (2005). Effects of teacher organization on classroom functioning. *Journal of School Psychology, 43*(1), 61–85.

Canva. (n.d.). Retrieved from https://www.canva.com/

CAST. (2018). *Universal Design for Learning Guidelines version 2.2*. Retrieved from http://udlguidelines.cast.org

Castek, J., Henry, L., Coiro, J., Leu, D., & Hartman, D. (2015). Research on instruction and assessment in the new literacies of online research and comprehension (p. 324–344). In S. Parris & K. Headley, *Comprehension instruction: Research-based best practices* (3rd ed., pp. 324–344). New York, NY: Guilford Press.

Center for Distributed Learning. (2012). *What is accessibility?* Teaching Online Website. Retrieved from https://cdl.ucf.edu/teach/accessibility/

Chen, B., Vargas, J., Thompson, K., & Carter, P. (2014). Screencasts. In B. Chen, A. deNoyelles, & K. Thompson (Eds.), *Teaching online pedagogical repository*. University of Central Florida Center for Distributed Learning. Retrieved from https://topr.online.ucf.edu/screencasts/

Clinton, J., & Dawson, G. (2018). Enfranchising the profession through evaluation: A story from Australia. *Teachers and Teaching, 24*(3), 312–327.

Conrad, P. (1994). *Prairie visions: The life and times of Solomon Butcher*. New York, NY: HarperCollins.

Conroy, M. A., Sutherland, K. S., Snyder, A. L., & Marsh, S. (2008). Classwide interventions: Effective instruction makes a difference. *TEACHING Exceptional Children, 40*(6), 24–30.

Consalvo, A., & Maloch, B. (2015). Keeping the teacher at arm's length: Student resistance in writing conferences in two high school classrooms. *Journal of Classroom Interaction, 50*(2), 120–132.

Cornelius-White, J. (2007). Learner-centered teacher-student relationships are effective: A meta-analysis. *Review of Educational Research, 77*, 113–143.

Cotton, K. (2001). *Classroom questioning.* North West Regional Educational Laboratory. Retrieved from https://educationnorthwest.org/sites/default/files/resources/classroom-questioning-508.pdf

Covey, S. (2008). *The speed of trust: The one thing that changes everything.* New York, NY: Simon & Schuster.

Davies, M., Kiemer, K., & Meissel, K. (2017). Quality talk and dialogic teaching: An examination of a professional development programme on secondary teachers' facilitation of student talk. *British Educational Research Journal, 43*(5), 968–987.

Elliott, K. W., Elliott, J. K., & Spears, S. G. (2018). Teaching on empty. *Principal, 98*(2), 28–29.

Elwell, L., & Lopez Elwell, C. (2020). That's not his name no more. *Leadership, 49*(3), 12–15.

Emmer, E. T., Evertson, C. M., & Anderson, L. M. (1980). Effective classroom management at the beginning of the school year. *The Elementary School Journal, 80*(5), 219–231.

Erdogan, I., & Campbell, T. (2008). Teacher questioning and interaction patterns in classrooms facilitated with differing levels of constructivist teaching practices. *International Journal of Science Education, 30*(14), 1891–1914.

Ericsson, A., & Pool, R. (2016). *Peak: Secrets from the new science of expertise.* Boston, MA: Houghton Mifflin Harcourt.

Evertson, C. M., & Emmer, E. T. (1982). Preventive classroom management. In D. Duke (Ed.), *Helping teachers manage classrooms* (pp. 2–31). Alexandria, VA: ASCD.

Fendick, F. (1990). *The correlation between teacher clarity of communication and student achievement gain: A meta-analysis* (Doctoral dissertation). Retrieved from University of Florida Digital Collections, https://ufdc.ufl.edu/AA00032787/00001

Figley, C. R. (2002). Compassion fatigue: Psychotherapists' chronic lack of self-care. *Journal of Clinical Psychology, 58*(11), 1433–1441.

Fisher, D., Frey, N., Amador, O., & Assof, J. (2019). *The teacher clarity playbook: A hands-on guide to creating learning intentions and success criteria for organized, effective instruction.* Thousand Oaks, CA: Corwin.

Fisher, D., Frey, N., & Hattie, J. (2016). *Visible learning in literacy.* Thousand Oaks, CA: Corwin.

Fisher, D., Frey, N., & Lapp, D. (2009). *In a reading state of mind: Brain research, teacher modeling, and comprehension instruction.* Newark, DE: International Reading Association.

Fisher, D., Frey, N., & Pumpian, I. (2011). No penalties for practice. *Educational Leadership, 69*(3), 46–51.

Fisher, D., Frey, N., Quaglia, R. J., Smith, D., & Lande, L. L. (2018). *Engagement by design: Creating learning environments where students thrive.* Thousand Oaks, CA: Corwin.

Fisher, D., Frey, N., & Smith, D. (2020). *Teacher credibility and collective efficacy playbook.* Thousand Oaks, CA: Corwin.

Fitzpatrick, J. (2016). Pop-up pedagogy: Sharing resources and generating teachable moments with students. *Journal of Family & Consumer Sciences, 108*(1), 52–54.

Fredricks, J. A., Blumenfeld, P. C., & Paris, A. H. (2004). School engagement: Potential of the concept, state of the evidence. *Review of Educational Research, 74*(1), 59–109.

Frey, N., Fisher, D., & Gonzalez, A. (2013). *Teaching with tablets.* Alexandria, VA: ASCD Arias.

Frey, N., Fisher, D., & Hattie, J. (2018). *Developing assessment-capable visible learners: Maximizing skill, will, and thrill.* Thousand Oaks, CA: Corwin.

Good, T. (1987). Two decades of research on teacher expectations. *Journal of Teacher Education, 38*(4), 32–47.

Gordon, R. (2004). The social system as a site of disaster impact and resource for recovery. *Australian Journal of Emergency Management, 19*(4), 16–22.

Gregory, K. (1997). *Across the wide and lonesome prairie: The diary of Hattie Campbell.* New York, NY: Scholastic.

Hall, R. M., & Sandler, B. R. (1982). *The classroom climate: A chilly one for women?* Retrieved from https://files.eric.ed.gov/fulltext/ED215628.pdf

Hattie, J. (2018). *250 Influences chart.* Retrieved from https://www.visiblelearning.com/content/visible-learning-research

Hattie, J., & Timperley, H. (2007). The power of feedback. *Review of Educational Research, 77*(1), 81–112.

Hattie, J., & Zierer, K. (2018). *10 mindframes for Visible Learning: Teaching for success.* New York, NY: Routledge.

Hendrickx, M. M. H. G., Mainhard, T., Oudman, S., Boor-Klip, H. J., & Brekelmans, M. (2017). Teacher behavior and peer liking and disliking: The teacher as a social referent for peer status. *Journal of Educational Psychology, 109*(4), 546–558.

Levin, T., & Long, R. (1981). *Effective instruction.* Alexandria, VA: ASCD.

Loom. (n.d.). Retrieved from https://www.loom.com/

Ma, W., Adesope, O. O., Nesbit, J. C., & Liu, Q. (2014). Intelligent tutoring systems and learning outcomes: A meta-analysis. *Journal of Educational Psychology, 106*, 901–918

Matsumura, L. C., Slater, S. C., & Crosson, A. (2008). Classroom climate, rigorous instruction and curriculum, and students' interactions in urban middle schools. *Elementary School Journal, 108*(4), 293–312.

Mehrabian, A. (1971). *Silent messages.* Belmont, CA: Wadsworth.

Mohr, K. A. J. (1998). Teacher talk: A summary analysis of effective teachers' discourse during primary literacy lessons. *Journal of Classroom Interaction, 33*(2), 16–23.

Nystrand, M., Gamoran, A., & Carbonaro, W. (1998). Towards an ecology of learning: The case of classroom discourse and its effects on writing in high school English and social studies (No. 11001). Albany, NY: National Research Center on English Learning & Achievement.

Nystrand, M., Wu, M., Gamoran, A., Zeiser, S., & Long, D. (2001). *Questions in time: Investigating the structure and dynamics of unfolding classroom discourse* (No. 14005). Albany, NY: The National Research Center on English Learning & Achievement.

O'Dell, S. (1970). *Sing down the moon.* Boston, MA: Houghton Mifflin.

Osofsky, J. D., Osofsky, H. J., & Harris, W. W. (2007). Katrina's children: Social policy considerations for children in disasters. *Society for Research in Child Development, 21*(1), 3–18.

Palincsar, A. S., & Brown, A. L. (1984). Reciprocal teaching of comprehension-fostering and comprehension-monitoring activities. *Cognition and Instruction, 1*(2), 117–175.

Palmer, D., Dixon, J., & Archer, J. (2016). Using situational interest to enhance individual interest and science-related behaviours. *Research in Science Education, 47*, 731–753.

Pane, J. F., McCaffrey, D. F., Kalra, N., & Zhou, A. J. (2008). Effects of student displacement in Louisiana during the first academic year after the hurricanes of 2005. *Journal of Education for Students Placed at Risk, 13*(2/3), 168–211.

PechaKucha 20x20. (n.d.). Retrieved from https://www.pechakucha.com/

Pfifferling, J., & Gilley, K. (2000). Overcoming compassion fatigue. *Family Practice Management, 7*(4), 39–44.

Pixabay. (n.d.). Retrieved from https://pixabay.com/

Porche, D. J. (2009). *Emergent leadership during a natural disaster: A narrative analysis of an acute health care organization's leadership* (Doctoral dissertation). Capella University. Retrieved from https://pqdtopen.proquest.com/doc/305162131.html?FMT=AI&pubnum=3378903

Priniski, S. J., Hecht, C. A., & Harackiewicz, J. M. (2018). Making learning personally meaningful: A new framework for relevance research. *Journal of Experimental Education, 86,* 11–29.

Randolph, J. J. (2007). Meta-analysis of the research on response cards: Effects on test achievement, quiz achievement, participation, and off-task behavior. *Journal of Positive Behavior Interventions, 9*(2), 113–128.

Rosenshine, B. (2008). *Five meanings of direct instruction.* Lincoln, IL: Center on Innovation & Improvement.

Ryan, P. M. (1998). *Riding freedom.* New York, NY: Scholastic.

Sacerdote, B. (2012). When the saints go marching out: Long-term outcomes for student evacuees of Hurricanes Katrina and Rita. *American Economic Journal: Applied Economics, 4*(1), 109–135.

Shomoossi, N. (2004). The effect of teachers' questioning behavior on EFL classroom interaction: A classroom research study. *The Reading Matrix, 4*(2), 96–104.

South Australia Department for Education and Child Development. (2019). *Transforming tasks: Designing tasks where students do the thinking.* Office for Education. Retrieved from https://acleadersresource.sa.edu.au/features/transforming-tasks/Transforming_tasks_overview_chart.pdf

Staarman, J. K. (2009). The joint negotiation of ground rules: Establishing a shared collaborative practice with new educational technology. *Language and Education, 23*(1), 79–95.

Stamm, B.H. (2010). *The Concise ProQOL Manual* (2nd ed.). Pocatello, ID: ProQOL.org.

Stanovich, K. E. (1986). Matthew effects in reading: Some consequences of individual differences in the acquisition of literacy. *Reading Research Quarterly, 22,* 360–407.

Van der Kolk, B. (2015). *The body keeps the score: Brain, mind, and body in the healing of trauma.* New York, NY: Penguin.

von Frank, V. (2010). Trust matters: For educators, parents, and students. *Tools for Schools, 14*(1), 1–3.

Voerman, L. A., Meijer, P., Korthagen, F., & Simons, R. P. (2012). Types and frequencies of feedback interventions in classroom Interaction in secondary education. *Teaching & Teacher Education, 28*(8), 1107–1115.

Wiliam, D. (2020). Formative assessment and online teaching. *Australian Institute for Teaching and School Leadership.* Retrieved from https://www.aitsl.edu.au/secondary/comms/australianteacherresponse/formative-assessment-and-online-teaching

Wangberg, J. K. (1996). Teaching with a passion. *American Entomologist, 42*(4), 199–200.

Windschitl, M. (2019). Disciplinary literacy versus doing school. *Journal of Adolescent & Adult Literacy, 63*(1), 7–13.

Wisniewski, B., Zierer, K., & Hattie, J. (2020). The power of feedback revisited: A meta-analysis of educational feedback research. *Frontiers in Psychology, 10,* 1–14.

Zierer, K., Lachner, C., Tögel, J., & Weckend, D. (2018). Teacher mindframes from an educational science perspective. *Educational Sciences, 8*(4), 209–221.

Zumbrunn, S., Marrs, S., & Mewborn, C. (2016). Toward a better understanding of student perceptions of writing feedback: A mixed methods study. *Reading & Writing, 29*(2), 349–370.

INDEX

CORWIN

A SAGE Publishing Company

Helping educators make the greatest impact

CORWIN HAS ONE MISSION: to enhance education through intentional professional learning.

We build long-term relationships with our authors, educators, clients, and associations who partner with us to develop and continuously improve the best evidence-based practices that establish and support lifelong learning.

CORWIN

Supporting TEACHERS | Empowering STUDENTS

THE TEACHER CLARITY PLAYBOOK

Designed for PLCs or independent teacher use, this playbook guides practitioners to align lessons, objectives, and outcomes of learning seamlessly, so that the classroom hours flow productively for everyone.

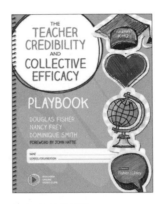

THE TEACHER CREDIBILITY AND COLLECTIVE EFFICACY PLAYBOOK

Jumpstart learning and achievement in your classroom by increasing your credibility with students and the collective efficacy of the team of educators at your school.

DEVELOPING ASSESSMENT-CAPABLE VISIBLE LEARNERS

Imagine students who understand their educational goals and monitor their progress. This illuminating book focuses on self-assessment as a springboard for markedly higher levels of student achievement.

PLC+

What makes a powerful and results-driven professional learning community (PLC)? The answer is *PLC+*, a framework that leads educators to question practices, not just outcomes.

THE PLC+ PLAYBOOK

Help your PLC+ group to work wiser, not harder, with this practical guide to planning and implementing PLC+ groups in a collaborative setting.

THE PLC+ ACTIVATOR'S GUIDE

The PLC+ Activator's Guide offers a practical approach and real-life examples that show activators what to expect and how to navigate a successful PLC journey.

Learn more at Corwin.com

Unleash the promise of social learning

No longer is professional learning confined to a specific time or place. With Corwin virtual professional learning, **PD can be everywhere and anywhere you need it.**

Corwin's virtual professional learning options give schools and districts the power to rapidly re-establish professional learning as a critical support to teachers during challenging times and offer flexible ways to engage with peers around urgent problems of practice.

CORWIN Visible Learning+™

Focus on Student Learning

Knowing our impact on students is the cornerstone of Professor John Hattie's research findings. The best laid instructional plans put student learning and teacher impact at the forefront. Focus on student feedback and developing student independence and resilience so that students can monitor their own progress and take ownership of their learning.

CORWIN Teacher Clarity

Get Clear on Instruction

Support teachers in how to provide instruction that is engaging and targeted to student needs. Teachers need clarity on how to best assess where students are in the fall, determine the focus of instructional units, and provide students what they need in meaningful and authentic ways. This is the foundation of effective teaching.

CORWIN PLC+

Rally Your Teachers

Your teachers are your greatest asset. Provide them the structures and processes to collaborate effectively to develop solutions to our most urgent problems of practice. This is a critical first step to ensure teachers work together effectively to support students in the most meaningful way.

PLSN20676

Learn more about our virtual PD options at **corwin.com/virtualpd**